A HOLY TRADITION OF WORKING

A Holy Tradition
of Working

Passages from the writings of
ERIC GILL

Introductory essay by
BRIAN KEEBLE

Foreword by
WALTER SHEWRING

THE LINDISFARNE PRESS
West Stockbridge · Massachusetts ·

Published by
THE LINDISFARNE PRESS
R.D. 2, West Stockbridge, MA 01266

© Golgonooza Press 1983

ISBN 0 940262 04 5

Library of Congress Catalogue
Card Number: 83 81565

Printed in the United Kingdom
by Skelton's Press Ltd
Wellingborough, Northamptonshire

Contents

Foreword

I specially welcome this anthology because it is built round that part of Eric Gill's thought which at the end of his life was at once most important to himself and least often grasped by those who read him or heard him speak – his doctrine of art in all its varieties as the normal pattern of human workmanship.

His last days, indeed, found him concerned with much else, in particular with pacifism, which in this book appears only fleetingly. But of that theme he was far from being the first or chief exponent; he joined, rather late in his life, a movement begun long before and entered now not only by individual writers but by great bodies of men and women working together and much perplexing the governments of the Right and Left. Nothing comparable has happened as regards his teaching on work. Many see him as their ally in the struggle of poor against rich or workers against capitalists, yet understand no better than their opponents what his true terms of reference are. When he says that work should be human, they think of the human thing as whatever satisfies themselves. When he says that work should be holy, they are bewildered.

So although the theme is human work, human making, we must begin much further back. What is man? What is in man? What is above man? If work means making things, how and why does the making take place? What is it for?

Brian Keeble in his essay has been well advised to remind the reader of some of Gill's predecessors in England who defied the conventions of their time in their ideas of man and work. Blake stands apart from the rest, and the verse here quoted on the Industrial Revolution is magnificent and poignant. The other writers, who all saw something and all missed something, have for some time past been little read, but for that very reason are rightly remembered here.

Beyond English frontiers, the pronouncements of successive popes from Leo XIII onwards, though given no rapid response from their flocks in general, were an encouragement and a consolation to Gill. 'This man', said Pius XII, looking up from a book of Gill's (I wish I knew which), 'this man has understood our encyclicals.' And a recent message of Pope John Paul reinforces Gill: It is true in one sense that man is meant for work; in a more important sense, work is meant for man.

Part of Gill's thought matured early, part awaited development. Much in his early essays always remained valid for him and ought to be valid for ourselves; certain things needed a modification or restatement which they received in his last years; a few imperfections of argument were never resolved at all.

In his ordinary dealings with others (for instance, with imperceptive clients) he was a quite remarkably patient man, but times came when his patience snapped. He could argue closely; but in certain arguments with himself his inward patience gave way too early and he came out with a makeshift answer to a difficulty. His followers ought to acknowledge this, and it is no bad thing that among the passages printed here should be a very short-sighted one on 'abstract' art and especially 'abstract' music (here VIII:2). This is modified – in part it is contradicted – by later passages in the same essay (e.g. VIII:8 here), but even so it reveals a struggle between his own experience and the task of reshaping a theory to meet it. He did in fact enjoy Bartok and Stravinsky, and had no qualms about playing a Bach prelude or a Frescobaldi *corrente* on his own eighteenth-century clavichord. His mental burden in this matter would certainly have been lightened had he lived to read the demonstration by

Marco Pallis* of how, for instance, a string quartet may be both rhetorical and didactic in the ancient and honourable sense of those words.

His main message I leave to this anthology, but I should like to recall one episode in his working life which illumines, I think, his teaching and his practice. David Jones agreed with me that the finest of all post-mediaeval works in Oxford was perhaps the War Memorial of 1921 in New College. Three things have been brought together there. First, the impersonal grandeur of the capitals has an appeal not unlike that of 'abstract' painting; then, its 5,000 or so letters are a factual, social and historical record of the more than two hundred members of the College who died in the first World War; then, this is the achievement not of one man of genius but of a master and some half-dozen pupils co-operating in one workshop.

I must add something on his manner of writing. He often wrote hastily and in difficult conditions, but when he had relative leisure and tranquillity he was, I think, one of the best writers of the century. Time after time, as I re-read the *Autobiography*, I am reminded of Dickens – not the jaded and clumsy writer of *Hard Times* but the natural, alert and sensitive writer of the second chapter of *David Copperfield*. And I doubt if any English novelist of today could equal the moving paragraph quoted here from *The Necessity of Belief* (XIV:11).

He has often been reproached with repetitiveness. I myself accept this trait in him as cheerfully as in Matthew Arnold. (What I do find embarrassing is an occasional Victorian facetiousness which I think was inherited.) And perhaps such repetitiveness in him was a natural reaction to the continued incomprehension of his audiences. In particular, the belief that the main purpose of work can only be

* 'Metaphysics of Musical Polyphony' chapter VIII in *A Buddhist Spectrum* (London, 1980) pp 121–128.

a profit in cash has so firmly taken root among both exploiters and exploited that many could not believe their ears when they heard a man denying this.

One authentic reminiscence. I was once at a lecture on art and industry in which he set forth his accustomed views. There were many business men in the audience, and the chairman was a business man. When the lecture ceased and the chairman rose, I awaited an explicit protest, mild or savage, against views so plainly hostile to the commercial world. But no. We should all, the chairman said, follow Mr. Gill's advice to put some art into industry; and after that, 'At the end of the year, when a man meets his accountant, he will find that he has not served his God in vain.'

WALTER SHEWRING

Acknowledgements

Grateful acknowledgement is made to the following publishers who have given permission to quote from their published material. To George Allen & Unwin Ltd for *The Hindu View of Art* by Mulk Raj Anand. To Barrie & Jenkins Ltd for *Edward Johnston* by Priscilla Johnston. The Bodley Head for *Art and a Changing Civilisation* by Eric Gill. Jonathan Cape Ltd and Devin Adair (N.Y.) for *Autobiography, Letters* and Jonathan Cape Ltd for *Clothes, In a Strange Land, Last Essays* by Eric Gill. Collier Macmillan Ltd for *Art Nonsense and other Essays* by Eric Gill. J. M. Dent Ltd for *Sacred and Secular, Work & Property* and *Typography* by Eric Gill. Faber & Faber for *Money and Morals, The Necessity of Belief* and *Work and Leisure* by Eric Gill. Oxford University Press for *Form in Civilisation* by W. R. Lethaby. Princeton University Press for *Selected Papers Volume I on Traditional Art and Symbolism* by A. K. Coomaraswamy. The Society for Promoting Christian Knowledge for *Christianity and the Machine Age* by Eric Gill. Sheed and Ward for *Beauty Looks After Herself* by Eric Gill and *Art and Scholasticism* by Jacques Maritain. I would also like to thank Ray Wilson and the staff of the Suffolk College Library for their help in obtaining many inaccessible items, Mrs Jane Collin for her patience and perseverance at the typewriter, Kathleen Raine, Philip Sherrard and Walter Shewring for saving me from a number of errors and for their constructive comments, and finally my printer Christopher Skelton for his moral and material support.

Abbreviations

The following abbreviated titles of Eric Gill's books are used throughout this book in conjunction with their page number(s).

ACC   *Art in a Changing Civilisation* 1934
AN   *Art Nonsense and other Essays* 1929
AR   'Art and Reality' in *The Hindu View of Art*
      by Mulk Raj Anand 1933
AU   *Autobiography* 1940
BLH   *Beauty Looks After Herself* 1933
CL   *Clothes* 1931
CMA   *Christianity and the Machine Age* 1940
DL   *Drawings from Life* 1940
ISL   *In a Strange Land* 1944
LE   *Last Essays* 1942
LT   *Letters of Eric Gill* (edited by Walter Shewring) 1947
MM   *Money and Morals* 1937
NB   *The Necessity of Belief* 1936
SS   *Sacred and Secular* 1940
TY   *An Essay on Typography* 1931
WL   *Work and Leisure* 1935
WP   *Work and Property* 1937

Introductory

Eric Gill was born on February 22nd, 1882 at Brighton. A talent for drawing led him to Chichester Art School, after which he was apprenticed to a London architect. Under the influence of W. R. Lethaby and Edward Johnston he took up letter carving, receiving his first commission in 1901. In 1913 Gill and his wife entered the Catholic Church, by his own admission the most important event in his life. With Hilary Pepler he formed a Craft Guild Community at Ditchling (1916–24). For four years he had his workshop at Capel-y-ffin in the Welsh Black Mountains. His final workshop community was at 'Pigotts' near High Wycombe from 1928 to 1940, the year of his death. In everything he did he was concerned to know and to live sacred principles common to man and the matter of human work. Those who knew him intimately attest to the integrity of vision and wisdom with which he realised his intention.

When Gill died at the age of 58 he left behind a dozen or so books and many shorter polemical writings, over a thousand wood-engravings, nine typeface designs, a considerable amount of sculpture, stone and wood carvings, inscriptions, some of the finest nude studies of this century, as well as designs for postage stamps, coins, books, at least one clock, a church and much else besides. No wonder that those who have written about him since cannot agree in their judgement as to the most enduring part of this legacy. About this perhaps Gill had his own ideas. David Jones reports that Gill had once said to him: 'What I achieve as a sculptor is of no consequence – I can only be a beginning – it will take generations, but if only the beginnings of a reasonable, decent, holy tradition of work might be effected – that is the thing.' Moreover, his friend and mentor Ananda K. Coomaraswamy wrote, '. . . he invented a human way of working, and found that it was that of all human societies . . . This amounts to saying that Eric's was not a personal point of view, but simply a true one, that he had made his own. He was not "thinking for himself" but assenting to credible propositions; and he was, accordingly, a man of faith.' There is a precedent then for pointing to Gill's doctrine of the norm of workmanship as the most singular part of his achievement.

Since his death, none of Gill's books has been reprinted. This has not deterred his critics, a good many of whom have had their own ideas of what he stood for. There is almost a folklore – in which fact and fiction are knit together – surrounding the memory of the man. Few bother to find out what he actually said. There is a consistent and coherent doctrine scattered among his writings. It needs extraction. This anthology attempts to present that philosophy essentially and integrally rather than exhaustively. It is time, once again, for Gill to have his say.

Eric Gill was all of a piece. You must take him whole or not at all. You can no more detach his doctrine of art from his doctrine of work than you can detach his morals from his religion. They all go together. He cannot be tried against the prevailing conditions or the 'inevitability of history' or against the acceptance of human culpability without those things thereby being seen the more clearly for what they are. His appeal is always to necessity and good sense.

Almost invariably, his past detractors have failed to perceive the level at which his thought moves. This failure on the part of many of his critics springs not so much from a mere disagreement about the purpose and direction of our civilisation as from their unwillingness to accept the degree to which Gill's views are at one and the same time 'absolute' and 'radical'.

Gill refused to put together a philosophy by way of small adjustments and accommodations to any of the modes and disguises with which the doctrine of a godless scientific and economic progress infiltrates the mental and physical life of modern society. Perhaps the more common form of capitulation to this 'progress' is the passive acceptance with which it is believed that 'machines are here to stay!' That Gill saw no such necessity, and that he saw their eventual demise as being due to their fundamental incompatibility with the proper nature of man has caused some of his critics to accuse him of wanting to go back to the middle ages. This criticism persists in spite of the fact that he has specifically written that there can be no putting back of the clock (XII:16) and that we must make the best of modern conditions on the basis of sheer reasonableness (XIV:8). Where the critic wants the convenience of what is familiar, and the compensations of 'art', Gill simply wants truth and consistency. Gill had his sights on the heavenly Jerusalem: his critics have theirs on England today, or perhaps tomorrow. It is the perpetual clash of interests between the politics of eternity and the politics of time.

This clash of interests, having engaged Gill's critics in the past, must certainly engage his reader today. There have been two permanent stumbling-blocks between Gill and his reader. The two interlock. The first is the obvious need to come to terms with the absoluteness of his image of man: his quite literal belief in the *fact* that man is created in the image of God. If you believe this to be true, and you examine the consequences that follow from it as rigorously as Gill did, your conclusions as to the nature and purpose of human life must be totally different from those you would hold if you believe that man is a mere 'higher', more clever primate, a more or less haphazard system of appetites, instincts and energy drives and the like. This latter view is so obviously incompatible with the whole spectrum of Gill's thought that the reader must either learn to accommodate

Gill on this point or admit that he desires other things and pass on.

The second stumbling-block – the assumption that the 'progress' of technological development is inevitable – we have already touched upon. But the following must be added. If you assume that the whole of man's experience does not go beyond the world of time and space then you must believe that all development will take place within the confines of that world. In which case there can only be an exploration of the extent of space and – since the horizontal movement of time is ever forward – development in future time. The pull of the future must seem inevitable in such circumstances. It is hardly coincidental, therefore, that the philosophy of materialism (which rests upon such assumptions) should, as Gill says, 'click' with an industrial world, and that in the nature of things it must issue in an ever greater degree of technological sophistication. But this did not prevent Gill from seeing the inconsistency of such a belief with free-will (with its concomitant of intellectual responsibility), and with the ultimate spiritual nature of man.

The two presiding principles along which, as it were, Gill guides his thoughts on the nature and purpose of human making are those of 'beauty' and 'art'. Let us look at his notion of beauty first. Here Gill's point of departure is St Thomas, quoting St Dionysios the Areopagite: 'The Beauty of God is the cause of all the being that is.' Thus beauty is an absolute and has to do with cognition. Absolute Beauty is the very cause of the perfection of things and as being is coincident with the Good, is the end to which the nature of things tends. The Scholastic doctrine of beauty as a transcendental, an objective property in things – the splendour of intelligibility – can be traced back through St Dionysios and Augustine to Plotinus and eventually to Plato's formulation of beauty as the radiance of truth. It was this tradition that St Thomas built upon but giving beauty a more immediate and subjective emphasis when he described it as 'that which pleases when seen'. But we must not assume that St Thomas's deceptively simple description identifies beauty with that pleasure, that quickening of the aesthetic senses that is felt in common delight. Gill reminds us that what *sees* is the mind, the 'inner eye' of the mind. Though the outward senses are the channel through which what pleases must pass, nevertheless in seeing beauty the mind acts and apprehends in the selfsame act Being Itself. In that act the thing that presents itself is not diffused or dissolved away into abstraction. It remains in the perfection and order proper to itself, a thing of greater clarity, a thing without which no beauty is seen at all. And this perfection and clarity is nothing less than the thing's essence, its form, the qualitative imprint, as it were, stamped on the created thing by its creator. Thus in the measure that a thing seen reflects the beauty proper to itself, so the mind sees what that thing is without adulteration and privation.

By analogy the same is true of works of art as things made, since whatever is made is first conceived in the mind of the artist. It is the intelligibility of this formative process in which the work of art is made in imitation of its mental prototype that the beauty of art consists. Just as the beauty of natural things is in accordance with the perfection of their being as part of the whole of the created order of things, so the beauty of a work of art is inseparable from its occasion and purpose as a thing called forth by intelligible need. Beauty cannot be said to be a property belonging to works of art exclusively, and the artist or workman does not proceed directly to 'make beauty' any more than he works to 'produce pleasure'. The beauty of works of art is not aesthetic (as is our pleasure at the resultant thing), but cognitive and in accordance with the goodness and truth with which the said work fulfils what it is its nature to be.

For this reason a work of art (or nature) is inseparable from its creator's intention, always remembering that as it is not part of God's intention to create natural things for the sake of idle curiosity, but to lead us on to higher things, so it should never be the intention of the artist to create meaningless luxuries which it is beneath man's natural dignity to tolerate.

The complementary principle to beauty in Gill's thought is that of art. Traditionally and normally, the notion of art is part of a body of wisdom according to which things made attain to the proper perfection of their nature (see IV:3). Man, considered in the light of an inverse metaphysical analogy whereby he is the reflected image of God, in fashioning an object materially at the same time fashions himself spiritually. By the same process of analogy in the act of creating God externalises Himself, whereas the artist or workman in the act of making internalises himself – by making outwardly, in an act of pure worship, man fashions his own internal essence. That is to say, he returns to the perfection of his own nature. Here we have the perennial idea of human vocation as part of the conformity of all things to their true nature as an expression of the divine will. Only he can attain perfection who is integrated with the causes and ends of things. This way he incurs no sin – sin being defined as a departure from the order to the end. We might recall that in his *Republic* Plato described justice as the freedom of men to do and act according to what it is their nature to be. (See VI:10.) And in connection with works of art Gill wrote: 'We've got to make things *right*. Beauty consists in due proportion. We have got to give things the proportion that is *due* to them. It's a matter of justice.' (LT200) The artist works, then, in imitation of the true nature of things. He does not imitate God's works, for that would be to make copies of copies, but imitates God's manner of working as it is inherent in his nature so to do.

The word 'art', in the scholastic formulation of the traditional wisdom, refers to that operative habit of the intellect by which the artist possesses what is the proper perfection of work to be done. This formulation takes as its point of departure Aristotle's description – in his *Ethics* (see IV:4) – of art as the innate condition of the mind by which a man proceeds upon a rational course of action in the making of something. Art is an inner skill, not mere outward dexterity. By the light of art the workman sees *what* is to be done; by the operation of art he knows *how* it shall be done. As the operative agent of art the workman's only concern is for the good of the work to be done. In departing from the perfecting of his art the workman sins *as an artist*. Art, then, stays in the artist and is not personified by the artist. David Jones observed of Gill that he worked as though a tradition existed. He meant that Gill worked assuming that these conditions and values both applied and were true.

With the division of 'art' from 'work' and 'beauty' from 'use' in the modern world, art comes *out* of the artist and gets attached, so to say, to the work of art itself. The creator of 'art', now called an 'artist', personifies art and is given the sole prerogative of its production. Beauty too comes out of the thing made to be an aesthetic sensation desired for its own sake. No longer the property of a thing that shows forth the fullness of integrity, harmony and intelligible clarity due to its being; no longer identified with goodness and truth, beauty is now associated with a select category of things made. As an aid to emotional stimulus, beauty is freed from the process of rational manufacture so that art has become 'pure' or 'fine' and as such is treated idealistically. The workman is no longer expected to be in *possession* of his art; 'art' and 'work' are distinct, even opposed, orders of making. Moreover, 'art' becomes a snob value and the word 'art' actually comes to denote the

objects that comprise this artificially isolated category of
things whose value is maintained in the interests of social
prestige. Indeed, the modern world speaks of 'art' instead
of 'works of art' because this artificial isolation makes it
necessary to distinguish 'art' from 'non-art' in the category
of things made.

All this Gill called 'art nonsense' and he sought to debunk
it in so far as it makes a 'false mysticism' of man's creative
spirit and distorts the proper order and status of intelligent
workmanship.

Gill's indebtedness to the English tradition of radical
thought, whose roots go back beyond William Cobbett to
Blake and reach forward through Carlyle, Ruskin, Morris
and on to his contemporaries and friends W. R. Lethaby
and Edward Johnston, has always been acknowledged.
Indeed, Gill's critique of the modern industrial world and
his re-affirmation of the dignity of human labour must be
set against the perspective of such thought as his achievement must be seen to be cumulative in respect of their
example.

Gill always acknowledged a degree of kinship with
William Blake, though he was far from sharing Blake's
visionary sense of the imagination. But just as Blake was the
prophet of the then industrialising English nation, so Gill
may yet be seen as the prophet of post-industrial England.
Blake was an artisan engraver in late 18th century London, a
time of decline in many such trades. The influx of population drifting away from agricultural subsistence in the
fields and villages of rural England had come to form the
mass of dispossessed and unskilled proletariat of the new
centres of mechanical production. In the wake of this
upheaval came the erosion of craft skills, and to Blake this
fact highlighted the destructiveness inherent in the process of mechanisation. Blake saw this process not indeed
primarily as destroying muscle and bone (though it did that

well enough) but as destructive of the inner man – *homo faber* – the 'Poetic Genius' in every man. 'A Machine is not a Man nor Work of Art; it is destructive of Humanity & of Art,' he declared in his *Public Address* of 1810. He had already, in about 1788, in his two tracts *There is no Natural Religion* and *All Religions are One*, found it necessary to point out that the nature of man is Infinite, in opposition to the encroaching philosophies of the mechanic system based exclusively upon a knowledge derived wholly from the bodily organs of perception. This bounded universe, as he saw, would be 'loathed by its possessor', for in denying man the Infinite that is connatural to him it binds him to the Ratio merely of his own ego.

In these tracts Blake settles once and for all the terms of reference for the ensuing radical debate on the destructiveness of the mechanical system. When Gill claims that 'death is the actual aim of industrialism, its diabolic direction', (XII : 11) it is nothing new. Blake had seen it a century earlier and had spoken out against it in a powerful passage in his *Jerusalem*:

> . . . all the Arts of Life they chang'd into the Arts of Death
>   in Albion.
> The hour-glass contemn'd because its simple workmanship
> Was like the workmanship of the plowman, & the water
>   wheel
> That raises water into cisterns, broken & burn'd with fire
> Because its workmanship was like the workmanship of the
>   shepherd;
> And in their stead, intricate wheels invented, wheel without
>   wheel,
> To perplex youth in their outgoings & to bind to labours in
>   Albion
> Of day & night the myriads of eternity; that they may grind
> And polish brass & iron hour after hour, laborious task,

Kept ignorant of its use: that they might spend the days of
   wisdom
In sorrowful drudgery to obtain a scanty pittance of bread,
In ignorance to view a small portion & think that All,
And call it Demonstration, blind to all the simple rules of
   life.

This passage anticipates a good deal of the thought Gill
expressed a century later after the same system had consistently proven its social and human divisiveness as well as
its spiritual impotence.

   Cobbett rode on horse-back over the southern counties
of the same England that Blake knew. A prodigious worker
himself, Cobbett knew the importance to a just society of a
right and responsible livelihood for its people. He wit-
nessed the rural aspect of the social upheaval created by the
drift of population to the 'Great Wen'. For him its effect was
not only social but was recognisable in the fact that it laid
waste the land. Cobbett had a hatred of unproductive land.
For him, where beauty and utility had been put asunder
there could be no natural beauty in a situation that was
morally unacceptable. He poured his inimitable scorn on
those responsible for the enclosure of the common land.
The consequent lack of ownership of the means of subsistence meant that the dispossessed agricultural labourer
was as much the slave of the 'Lords of the Loom' as was the
factory worker. Cobbett saw, and knew that he saw, the
germinating seeds of the modern consumer society. His
denunciation of the increasing self-sufficiency of the body
of 'idlers and traffickers' who create the modern market place,
keeping apart those who produce things and those who
have need of them, had its basis in the observation that, in
such conditions, both the producer and the consumer
must gradually relinquish control over the means of production in favour of the 'middle-men, who create nothing,

who add to the value of nothing, who improve nothing . . .
and who live well, too, out of the labour of the producer
and the consumer'. Cobbett was no less aware of the effect
of all this upon the mass of city slaves. Here his analysis of
the 'calamity' occasioned by the mechanic invention pre-
figures Gill's concern that the machine is only acceptable if
wholly owned and directed by the worker himself who
must also have the benefit of the profits that accrue to its
working: 'We must have the machine *at home* and we *ourselves* must have *the profit* of it; for, if the machine be *elsewhere*;
if it be worked *by other hands*; if *other persons* have the *profit* of
it . . . then the machine is an injury to us,' he wrote in his
Rural Rides.

Beyond recognising the dignity it may lend, and the injustice, when its fruits are withheld, that labour may
occasion man, Cobbett said little about the inherent nature
of work. But Thomas Carlyle went further. In the chapter
'Labour', in his *Past and Present*, he saw that 'there is a
perennial nobleness, and even sacredness in work'. Moreover, 'a man perfects himself by working', for 'even in the
meanest sorts of Labour, the whole soul of a man is com-
posed into a kind of real harmony.'

Carlyle saw into the centre of the active life of the working man. Recognising a sort of platonic justice there, he
wrote, 'Blessed is he who has found his work' for in 'the
inmost heart of the Worker rises a god-given Force.' For
him the only knowledge is that which holds good in working – the rest is 'hypothesis of knowledge'. In such thoughts
Carlyle comes close to expressing the traditional notion
of the marriage of wisdom and method in all vocational
endeavour – 'Admirable is that of the old Monks, "*Laborare
est Orare*, Work is Worship"' – a balance of the contemplative and active life of the intelligence and the will, the
harmony of reposed soul and dynamic body. In Carlyle we
have a foretaste of Gill's thought that as man is the summit

of nature, so his art improves on nature, and that every man
is a special kind of artist. In the same work Carlyle wrote,
'He that works, whatsoever be his work, he bodies forth the
form of Things Unseen; a small Poet every Worker is.' The
humblest platter, the Epic Poem, these that Nature has not
yet seen he creates – to Her a 'No-thing!' – these the worker
summons from the Unseen, 'in and for the Unseen'. He
who looks to the powers of this world must ever play at
the deceiving of his true self – the unspeaking voice of
conscience, the silent reverberation of perfection in his
nature. The worker who, for whatever reason, looks to 'the
world and its wages', works at a 'Sham-thing' which is best
not done. Thus Carlyle saw, before Ruskin, that the tragedy
of industrial work, 'under bondage to Mammon', was the
enforced idleness of 'the rational soul' it induced in the
worker, stopping the springs of charity and thus destroying
the moral basis of human intercourse.

If the ultimate nature of Carlyle's religious notions was
somewhat vague, there was no mistaking the 'true Deity' of
his age: 'Mechanism'. Under this secular god men no
longer feel the pull of the 'internal perfection'; their faith, as
he wrote in his essay 'Signs of the Times', is 'for external
combinations and arrangements, for institutions, consti-
tutions, – for Mechanism of one sort or other, do they hope
and struggle. Their whole efforts, attachments, opinions,
turn on mechanism, and are of a mechanical character.'

The well-springs of faith in the 'Deity of Mechanism' had
been pinpointed by Coleridge in his *Statesman's Manual* of
1816, some 13 years before the prophetic text of Carlyle's
essay. The mechanic philosophy, Coleridge wrote (elabo-
rating on Blake's tracts, as it were), 'demanding for every
mode and act of existence real or possible *visibility*, knows
only of distance and nearness, composition (or rather
juxtaposition) and decomposition, in short the relation
of unproductive particles to each other; so that in every

instance the result is the exact sum of the component quantities, as in arithmetical addition. This is the philosophy of death, and only of a dead nature can it hold good.' This 'philosophy of death', founded on the mechanism of Hobbes, the empiricism of Locke and the economics of Adam Smith, had issued in a 'commercial spirit, and the ascendancy of the experimental philosophy which . . . combined to foster its [the discursive understanding's] corruption. Flattered and dazzled by the real or supposed discoveries, which it had made, the more the understanding was enriched, the more did it become debased; till science itself put on a selfish and sensual character, and *immediate utility*, in exclusive reference to the gratification of the wants and appetites of the animal, the vanities and caprices of the social, and the ambition of the political, man was imposed as the test of all intellectual powers and pursuits. *Worth* was degraded in to a lazy synonym of *value*; and value was exclusively attached to the interest of the senses.'

Carlyle, in his moment of vision in 'Signs of the Times', caught an echo of the warning sounded by Coleridge: that the mechanical model by which men hoped to shape the world shapes man in its turn. Men come to conceive and understand themselves on the model of external circumstances. Cultivated on exclusively mechanical principles, the inward is finally abandoned and the mind is emptied of any significance other than that of evincing the mechanical method. This undue cultivation of the outward overrides and considers as nothing the 'Dynamic', as Carlyle called it, in man's nature: 'the primary, unmodified forces and energies of man, the mysterious springs of Love, and Fear, and Wonder, of Enthusiasm, Poetry, Religion, all which have a truly vital and *infinite* character.' More and more, development comes to mean something external and measurable; social virtues are equated with political and economic expediency. 'Men are to be guided only by their self-interests.' The cash nexus that binds the worker to his employer becomes the standard by which men measure all effort and reward. When the sufficiency and corruption of public laws prove their inability to maintain an effective balance of 'self-interests' – for it is the law of the new political economy that property should be concentrated and protected – exploitation comes as naturally as fruit to the tree.

With regard to the ethical neutrality of a system of manufacture in which work had atrophied to a mere mechanical function, Ruskin, as Gill acknowledged in his essay devoted to him, saw 'clearly that the roots of human action, and therefore of human art, are moral roots.' Just as, in the face of the rapid advance of the new system, Carlyle had found it necessary to point to the contrast between the 'Dynamical' and the 'Mechanic' Method, so Ruskin in his turn points to the moral contrast in the division of society inimical to the 'Mercantile Economy'; the economy of 'pay' signifies the legal, moral and social claims made by the few upon the labour of the many: poverty and debt on the one side, riches and right on the other. But for one who had seen that 'there is no wealth but life' the iniquities of the disproportion in reward between employer and employed were less important than those of a system that could manufacture anything 'except men'. It was not so much the division of labour or the 'degradation of the operative into a machine' that the system had achieved but the division of men themselves, 'broken into small fragments and crumbs of life', as he put it in *The Stones of Venice*.

Like Carlyle before him and Coomaraswamy and Gill a century later, Ruskin had glimpsed the truth that every man was a special kind of artist and thought the task of the reformer was to rekindle in every labourer that 'power for better things', the '*thoughtful* part' of him which must be prized and honoured even in its imperfection 'above the best and most perfect manual skill' such as the mechanic system produces. This way he would be 'made a man', whereas before he had been a mere 'animated tool'. In *Unto This Last* Ruskin had castigated his uncomprehending contemporaries for their unquestioning reliance upon the modern political economy itself built upon the premisses of Mill, Malthus, Ricardo, etc. What the new science had left out of account was precisely the 'motive power of the soul'. It was this very unacknowledged quality, the soul, that seeped into every quantitative calculation of the 'political economist's equations, without his knowledge, and falsifies every one of their results. Work is best done, not for pay or under pressure but 'only when the motive force, that is to say, the will or spirit of the creature, is brought to its greatest strength' by the 'social affections' – precisely what the political economist is likely to see as merely 'accidental and disturbing elements in human nature'. Blake, Coleridge, Carlyle, and then Ruskin, each struggled to keep open a sense of the soul's worth in the face of its gradual occlusion by the closed system that accepts as its sole province the domain of what can be measured and weighed.

But Ruskin, though he had seen that the work of mere utility – the 'dishonour of manual labour' – must be done away with altogether, showed the impotence with which Gill charged him when it came to the question of the beautiful. With the eye of an aesthete whose vision is formed on an inverted materialism he wrote in *Modern Painters*; 'Any material object which can give us pleasure in the simple contemplation of its outward qualities without any direct or definite exertion of the intellect, I call in some way, or in some degree, beautiful.' For Ruskin the beautiful was always something incidental, something added, like a sheen or gloss to the being of a thing, not a light within it.

Never a cognitive principle, beauty is always an affective impulse and is sensational as to its object. It is thus not surprising that 'art', for Ruskin, far from being the rational principle of normal workmanship, was not much more than whatever elicits his deepest feelings at delighted observation – and the artist is, for him, one who can depict such feelings. Attempting to unite beauty and workmanship, in a passage in *The Two Paths*, he wrote: 'Beautiful art can only be produced by people who have beautiful things about them, and leisure to look at them; and unless you provide some elements of beauty for your workmen to be surrounded by, you will find that no elements of beauty can be invented by them.'

William Morris's wrestling with the divisive monster of beauty on the one hand and utility on the other took a different form yet again from that of his predecessors. He saw through the fallacy of the Protestant ethic – used as an expedient to bridge the divide – that work, *any* work, because it serves 'the sacred cause of labour', is good in itself. This same fallacy Carlyle had come close to advocating. For Morris, the evil shadow of the industrialised system obscured the light of an obvious truth: there are, he wrote in *Useful Work Versus Useless Toil*, 'two kinds of work – one good, the other bad; one not far removed from a blessing, a lightening of life; the other a mere curse, a burden to life.' The work it was manly to do has hope in it, a threefold hope – 'hope of rest, hope of product, hope of pleasure in the work itself'. All other work 'is slave's work – mere toiling to live, that we may live to toil'. Such was the heritage of the dispossessed peasants of the 18th Century who became the proletariate of the 19th – 'a great mass of slaves, who must be fed, clothed, housed, and amused as slaves, and that their daily necessity compels them to make the slave-wares whose use is the perpetuation of their slavery.' This fact remained fundamental to Gill's view of contemporary society (XI:11). He too saw that the tyranny of the modern market place consists in the fact that the buyer, far from being an enlightened patron (which he could still in a measure be at the country fairs Cobbett saw must be destroyed by the increased trafficking of middle-men in shops), is no more in possession of an educated taste and discretion that any other consumer of those goods which are called into existence for no other reason than to serve as the very life-blood of the system of their production. For Morris the smart of injustice was in the enforced degradation of man at this 'tax of waste', this treadmill futility that is a trading on the ignorance of the productive masses by the profit-gathering minority who have 'the power of compelling other men to work against their will'. For Gill (who transposed many of Morris's observations into the terms of his own philosophy), no less than for Morris, this imposition upon the worker to labour against his will was by necessity inherent in the mechanical system; the necessity to destroy in the worker any real intellectual responsibility he might have for what he makes. As Morris put it in How We live and How We Might Live: 'they do not know what they are working at, nor whom they are working for, because they are combining to produce wares of which the profit of a master forms an essential part, instead of goods for their own use.' Moreover, 'they will be in fact just a part of the machinery for the production of profit; and so long as this lasts it will be the aim of the masters or profit-makers to decrease the market value of this human part of the machinery.' This is easily recog-nisable as the foundation of Gill's mature view of the question of the modern worker being merely the sentient part of the machine who has only his energies with which to trade his life and whose life must be put at its lowest acceptable value by his masters.

In seeking a solution to the redistribution of justice as

well as profit, like Ruskin before him, Morris was to founder on the rock of beauty, which was for him a sub-jective addition to life and its necessary utilities. Hence, as Morris supposed, if the worker is freed from the iniquities of a system that encroaches at every moment upon his work and his leisure time as well as his artistic and his moral accountability, he would make things at a sufficient pace of leisure that the work of his hands (it would come to this), in harmony with his pleasure at creation, would add beauty to his products. Thus would come about the 'pleasant life', a sort of paradise on Earth whose occupants would have; 'First, a healthy body; second, an active mind in sympathy with the past, the present, and the future; thirdly, occu-pation fit for a healthy body and an active mind; fourthly, a beautiful world to live in.'

Given Gill's integrated religious and metaphysical view-point, it was inevitable that he would come to reject this vaguely humanist dream of a paradise whose *raison d'être* is curiously absent: inevitable that he should see that Morris's politics were those of time and not of eternity. Gill, in judging Morris, applied the same principle as on so many occasions and went straight to the heart of the matter: 'He saw no being behind doing.' (NB304). Morris's pre-dominant concern was for the fact that, by the mechanical system, the workman is robbed of the pleasure and satis-faction of free creative effort, and a just reward for his labour. But Gill's concern was for the fact that the worker, in being robbed of intellectual responsibility, is also robbed of the possibility of apprehending the holiness of the creation and of his own being by means of a life of work as prayer; a norm of manufacture connatural to man's rational intelligence. Even though he was prepared to concede that art cannot flourish in the hands of a coterie of specially gifted men, Morris nonetheless thought that art must be the outcome of a vaguely humanistic aspiration towards what he called the 'beauty and true pleasure of life'. Despite his undoubted personal skills in the many crafts he practised, Morris had no proper doctrine of work. When he came to describe his vision of the social revolution he had called for – which revolution was no more than 'a stage of the great journey of evolution that joins the future and the past to the present,' – we find that vision trailing off into an increasingly attenuated generalisation: 'I console myself with visions of the noble communal hall of the future, unsparing of materials, generous in worthy ornament, alive with the noblest thoughts of our time, and the past, embodied in the best art which a free and manly people could produce.' The artist's role in the construction of such a society was to produce no more than 'beauty and interest'.

It is significant that both Ruskin and Morris believed that greater leisure and a higher standard of living would lead to the restitution of the arts among the people. By contrast Gill called for a 'holy poverty' (XIII:13) as the only rational attitude to material things; hence his criticism of Morris that 'he saw joy in labour but no sacrifice'. (NB304) What is more, Gill foresaw that in the Welfare State the 'factory hand' would come to despise the culture of 'higher things' for which he is supposedly made free by the mechanical system. (XIV:13)

Although he had learned much from Morris, Gill rejected him. It was as much a rejection of the Arts and Crafts movement as a whole as of Morris himself. Gill also rejected the socialism that went with their vision on the grounds that they had no effective answer to the system they affected to despise; a system which perpetuated the moral irresponsibility of the capitalist investor on the one hand and the intellectual irresponsibility of the worker on the other. (AU270) Whereas the Arts and Crafts movement had merely established a vogue among the rich for sentimentalism, socialism, because it had failed to see anything wrong in the industrial system of production as a solution to the problem of human need, as a political movement was, as Gill wrote, 'hardly more than an attempt to re-order the distribution of factory products and factory profits'. (AU140)

Of this failure of socialism it fell to Morris's disciple W. R. Lethaby to make the obvious point. Now that the conditions of labour had been bettered by the rise of Trade Union power – and seeing that mechanised production cannot form a sufficient basis for human conduct – the task of the Unions must be to attend to the 'element of quality in workmanship'. Indeed; 'As work is the first necessity of existence, the very centre of gravity of our moral system, so a proper recognition of work is a necessary basis for all right religion, art and civilisation. Society becomes diseased in direct ratio to its neglect and contempt of labour.' Like Carlyle, Ruskin and Morris, Lethaby too looked for his bearings to the unified tradition of art and workmanship that was the natural expression of the mind of the Middle Ages: 'The most distinctive characteristic of the Middle Ages was the honourable position in the State then taken up by labour.'

But Lethaby went one step further along the road uniting beauty and use, art and work, by being more explicit and concrete in his definitions. In Lethaby we find a good many of Gill's mature conclusions on the nature of beauty, art and workmanship, in at least a verbal form that is close to Gill's own. Indeed, it was Lethaby who wrote in his book on Architecture; 'we need not trouble about beauty, for that would take care of itself.' Among his papers on Art and Labour (published in 1922 as Form in Civilisation), are aphoristic distillations of thought that might almost have come from Gill's pen: 'Beauty is that which when seen we should love': 'Beauty is the "substance" of things done': 'Beauty is the flowering of labour and service': 'Beauty has to come by the way': 'Appreciation of Beauty should be one with our judgement of essential quality . . . The sense of Beauty is the work-conscience'.

For Lethaby, art is 'the right way of doing right things'. Art is 'ordinary manipulative skill'. It is *service* before it is delight; it is *labour* as well as emotion; it is *substance* as well as expression'. 'A work of art implies workmanship.' 'What I mean by art, then, is not the affair of a few but of everybody.'

Like Gill, Lethaby, theoretically at least, fused yet did not confuse art and utility. He was fully aware of the transcendental origins of human workmanship and had written widely on themes of myth, symbol and cult related to what he called in his essay 'The Centre of Gravity', 'the "revelation" of the crafts to men'. Gill, during his formative years, had been closely associated with Lethaby and would obviously have absorbed much of his teaching. Yet for all the similarity of Lethaby's final position to that of Gill in the theory of beauty, art and workmanship, there remains the feeling that it is just that: theory. We cannot find anything like the same degree of personal, manipulative as well as theoretic integrity in Lethaby that we find in the life and work of Gill. Although Lethaby could situate the proper place of beauty in art, art in workmanship and service, he lacks Gill's depth of resonance and conviction in being able to inter-relate spirit and matter, being and doing, man and society, art and utility, beauty and holiness to an adequate metaphysical structure. And this reservation could apply equally well to all but Blake of those precursors of Gill that we have examined. But to the list of Gill's masters there is one more name to be added. In some ways he is the most important of Gill's masters.

It was the mastery of Edward Johnston's calligraphy that first gave Gill a direct experience of what was meant by work conceived and executed out of the living unity of beauty and utility. The excitement of the experience was, he wrote, 'as of the intelligence discovering the good . . . and finding it desirable'. The aesthetic 'shock' at first seeing Johnston's writing transported the younger man: 'I was caught unprepared. I did not know such beauties could exist. I was struck as by lightning, as by a sort of enlighten-ment: . . . and for a brief second seemed to know even as God knows.' (AU119–20)

Much of what Gill himself was to absorb from Johnston's teaching remained axiomatic: *Making* refers to the material object, *doing* to action and intention; the worker is one who works in substances, and these substances demand a special method. Thus the substance impinges directly upon the form of the thing to be made. The worker thinks of substance, object and design as inseparable factors in the process of workmanship. The product of work is substance brought to life – and that which is thus brought to life is the very mark of the worker's being. The primary occasion of work is use. Good work is fit purpose. Use and purpose determine the proper treatment of the object. The worker aims at beauty only indirectly as attaining a measure of divine reward. Use and beauty define the axis of embodied truth – usefulness being the end most immediately and commonly apprehended. It is use that curbs the three sins to which the workman is prey; lack of resolve, meaningless imitation and affectation. Such thoughts of Johnston's, learned as the practical wisdom of human facture, lasted Gill all his life.

In an important passage in his *Autobiography* Gill makes a confession and in so doing makes an important and fundamental distinction, one that helps us to understand the complex process of absorption and rejection in his approach to his masters: 'my socialism was from the begin-ning a revolt against the intellectual degradation of the factory hands and the damned ugliness of all that capitalist-industrialism produced, and it was not primarily a revolt against the cruelty and injustice of the possessing classes or against the misery of the poor. It was not so much the working *class* that concerned me as the working *man* – not so much what he got from working as what he did by working.' (AU111) Thus, for all their concern at the social injustice of the mechanised system, for all that they had shown themselves sensitive to the archetype of beauty, arguing for its return at the heart of human labour in the face of the increasing dehumanisation of mechanical production, Gill's precursors had not got to the root of the matter. They had not questioned consistently, deeply and vigorously enough the nature of man's being.

It is Gill's insistence on starting nearly every argument with the implied question 'What is Man?' and following up with penetrating clarity its necessary and rational corollaries that distinguish him from his masters. In recovering the norm of human workmanship on the basis of the whole meaning of life Gill avoided the fallacy (one to which modern man is particularly prone) of attempting to establish the criteria for the active life in the productive outcome of the active life itself. The depth and conviction of Gill's achievement is present in virtue of his total response to the truth of those metaphysical doctrines he made his own but which were no less the possession of the perennial wisdom that at nearly all times and places has been the normal spiritual legacy of man.

What of Eric Gill today? It would be all too easy to dismiss him as a nostalgic reactionary who, in looking back to the ideals of an earlier age, placed himself out of court in so far as the problems of late 20th century society are concerned. But such a judgement would not only be superficial, it would also be wrong. Gill, by the absolute categories of his thought and by his constant appeal to reason placed himself at the centre of things. The problems that engaged his mind

are still with us. Far from being resolved, they have merely
been brought, in the years since his death, to a new level of
sophistry, becoming an unquestioned part of the social and
intellectual malaise. Time and again Gill thinks his way to
the root of those fallacies and contradictions upon which
modern society unwittingly rests: its social and productive
system that has mass leisure as one of its main aims yet
which leads to the 'tragedy' of state-sponsored idleness;
its sentimentalising of art while dehumanising work; its
pursuit of individualism by means that tend to even greater
conformity and standardisation; its denial of the place and
significance of the Infinite in a world expected to yield
'infinite' material development. Only those who have
capitulated to the premises on which the current social
and economic condition of society rests can afford the
specious luxury of seeing Gill as an outmoded figure.

There is now a growing body of opinion that would hold
that if the industrialised world is to recover its balance it can
only do so on the basis of a re-sacralisation of work such as
Gill points to. A system of production, fuelled by a morally
neutral capital investment that in turn fuels a technological
development which is itself blind in so far as the ultimate
goal of society is concerned, can give only the appearance
of justice (in improved conditions, higher salaries, etc.) not
the reality of it. The driving force of such a society, Gill saw,
can lend nothing to a vision of that final end from which
man must take the meaning of his existence. If the industrial
system frees man for 'higher things' by reducing his need to
labour, why must there be such an outcry at the consequences of paid unemployment? As Gill observes, slavery
may no more be necessarily uncomfortable than freedom
comfortable. (IX:1)

Gill's views on economics and politics have been criti-
cised as being naïve, presumably by those who would consider the economics of industrial production, with its

insatiable appetite for the Earth's resources (not to mention the attendant problems of wide-scale dereliction and pollution), enlightened. Simple and unaffected his views may have been, but never as if unacquainted with evil. Hence, in his observation that the machine is primarily an instrument for producing profits (XI:10) is foreshadowed the observation that the modern economy is primarily concerned to produce *demand.* In seeing the man of business as being at the mercy of 'undisciplined fancies' (XI:11), Gill recognised the remorseless circularity of that unique form of modern slavery, 'consumerism'. He saw that its victim, the 'consumer' – that final triumph of 'economic man' – has no choice but to roam the market place in order to squander the 'fee' paid him for the time spent supporting a system whose very existence depends upon contriving ways to stimulate a demand for goods that can never be wholly satisfied. Such is the treadmill of 'consumer choice' and hence it comes about that men must serve 'the Economy' for the good of a society that has no higher notion of the social good than that of 'free enterprise' serving consumer demand. Already, in *News from Nowhere,* Morris had spoken of the inevitable downward spiral whereby 'the production of measureless quantities of worthless makeshifts' knew no limit since 'the only admitted test of utility in wares was the finding of buyers for them – wise men or fools, as it might chance.' Producer and consumer alike, must come to suffer the smart of tyranny when 'the Economy' has the power of Holy Writ!

In the field of 'art', too, in so far as it is a separate and specialised domain of activity in modern society, Gill's views are no less timely. By insisting on the connatural nature of common sensibility and pure being in the intuition of beauty Gill effectively joined what had for some centuries been artificially separated: Being and knowing, loving and thinking, living and making. His assimilation of

beauty to truth and goodness, moreover, provides a path
between the twin (from the traditional viewpoint) heresies
of post-renaissance aesthetics. The first heresy was the
seemingly irreversible persuasion of some four hundred
years during which 'art' had taken the imitation of appearances as a yardstick for expression. The invention of
photography 'killed' this heresy, but the counter-measure
of the modern movement – an emphasis on the abstract
nature of aesthetic values – opened up an equal and opposite heresy. The heresy of naturalism falsifies the nature of
reality by tending to limit it to appearances, forgetting that,
logically, appearances are of something. The heresy of
abstraction falsifies the nature of intelligence in supposing
that reality is all in the delight the mind feels in its own
correspondence to certain values of pattern and symmetry.
It is perhaps not too difficult to see that behind these twin
heresies are two equally partial and unconscious theories
of the beautiful – at their crudest, the one exclusively
objective and the other exclusively subjective. In the objective view beauty is thought to reside in the appearance of
the things we perceive. In the subjective view the objective
reality of the thing perceived is granted but beauty is
thought to belong to the act of emotive assimilation. The
objective view will not accept that the act of perception is
adaptive and contributory in the assimilation of beauty
while the subjective view will not accept that beauty is not
wholly attributable to emotive response. In other words,
neither view can accept that beauty is in the order of being.
Both forms of heresy tend to overlook the fact that the
relationship between mind and beauty – utilising the simul-
taneous co-operation of both perception and emotion – is
ultimately cognitive and depends more upon the action of
the intellect than upon sensory stimulus. (See VI:3)

On the basis of Gill's doctrine we might notice how it is
hardly a coincidence that in a society which unwittingly

subscribes to the notion of art as the province of a special sort of person concerned with beauty, art eventually becomes that hypertrophied banality and crudity with which we are all too familiar. Indeed, a society which unconsciously holds that the pursuit of beauty is the purpose of 'art' results in an environment unsurpassed in its dehumanising ugliness; similarly, the pursuit of leisure as the basis of the good life results in a society in which few people find the time to make what is pleasing to our innate sense of what conforms to a good life.

There can be no mistaking the directional impulse of Gill's thought; it is heavenward. Not so much a heaven 'up there' as one with a more local habitation: the kingdom of heaven within, which is the kingdom proper to man – that is to man the maker.

*   *   *

I am well aware that the arrangement of the anthology is somewhat artificial but that is no more than a necessity of presentation. It is not, I hope, unfaithful to Gill. Many of the quotations could as effectively appear in places different from those in which they are now found. But it should be clear that this in no way indicates a confusion or weakness on Gill's part. Rather the opposite; it is precisely Gill's coherence of mind and action that makes it possible for the reader to explore the riches of cross referring from one extract to another.

As previously indicated, I have not tried here to represent every facet of Gill's thought, but have included only those statements that relate immediately, or are contextual to, his thoughts on the nature of art, beauty and workmanship. I have not even tried to represent every nuance of his thinking on these three questions. Nevertheless, I believe the whole of his doctrine of the norm of workmanship is essentially present and that any additions would only extend and elaborate ideas already included.

The repetitiveness of Gill's writings has obviously been greatly curtailed by such a method of presentation. But again, I have not deliberately sought to get rid of it altogether. Such a course would amount, in this case, to misrepresentation, for Gill's repetitions are a mark of the man, and in any case they were the fundamentals he thought should be repeated lest they be forgotten. Be that as it may, the simplicity and disarming directness of Gill's pen are indications of an enviable and undeviating clarity of will, heart and mind.

The editor's additions and excisions to the excerpts are all enclosed in square brackets. In the case of excisions where [. . .] appears in the paragraph it may be assumed that a short passage has been cut. Where [. . .] occurs between paragraphs a whole paragraph or even more has been cut. I have sometimes, without indicating it, dropped a single word at the beginning of an excerpt.

Bibliographical Note

Eric Gill has been the subject of three large scale studies. The first, *The Life of Eric Gill* by Robert Speaight (London, 1966) is an excellent biography marred by the author's inability to grasp, on several occasions, Gill's meaning. This leads him to make a number of hasty and unwarranted judgements. Donald Attwater's *A Cell of Good Living: The Life, Works and Opinions of Eric Gill* (London, 1969) is sound throughout and is the most faithful extended study of Gill so far. Malcolm Yorke's *Eric Gill, Man of Flesh and Spirit* (London, 1981) is the best study of Gill's actual works and contains many reproductions from all media. The author attempts a critical assessment of Gill's stature as an artist but is hampered in his unwillingness to free himself from 'art nonsense' and this makes the criteria of his assessment somewhat specious. For an extended review of this book see the present author's 'Looking Back on Eric Gill' in *Temenos* 3 (London, 1982) pp 175–83. The smaller, earlier monograph by Donald Attwater, *Eric Gill: Workman* (London, 1941) remains a reliable introduction to much of Gill's thought. I have made only an oblique acknowledgement in my footnotes to Gill's debt to the writings of A. K. Coomaraswamy and to Jacques Maritain's *Art et Scholastique*. Gill made the latter book and many of Coomaraswamy's papers and books so much his own that it would require an independent study to do justice to their interaction. Gill very often gives as his own view what is in fact a paraphrase of one of these two authors. Certainly any reader of Gill should not overlook Maritain's book, which is best read in the second English translation by J. F. Scanlan as *Art and Scholasticism with other Essays* (London, 1930). Not that Gill accepted Maritian's thought unquestioningly but any reader who feels the inclination to acquaint himself with traditional metaphysical doctrines – and strictly speaking these alone provide the proper context to Gill's thought – would do better to consult as a minimum, Coomaraswamy's *Christian and Oriental Philosophies of Art* (N.Y. 1956), *The Transformation of Nature in Art* (N.Y. 1956), and Coomaraswamy, *Selected Papers*, Vol. I. *Traditional Art and Symbolism* (Princeton, Bollingen Series, 1977). It was Gill's opinion of Coomaraswamy that 'no other living writer has written the truth in matters of art life and religion and piety with such wisdom and understanding.'

Among the most valuable scattered papers on Gill the reader may usefully consult the following: 'Created Holiness' by Kenelm Foster, O.P. in *Blackfriars* Vol. XXII (February, 1941) pp 74–81; and in the same issue 'Eric Gill's Social Principles' by Bernard Kelly pp 82–87; 'Eric Gill as Sculptor' and 'Eric Gill' by David Jones in *Epoch and Artist* (London, 1959) pp 288–302; 'Eric Gill: A Reply' by Walter Shewring in *Blackfriars* Vol. XXIX (May, 1948) pp 385–387; 'Considerations on Eric Gill' by Walter Shewring in *Making and Thinking* (London, 1956) pp 88–103; several of the other essays in this book are recommended to the reader's attention as being relevant to an understanding of Gill's thinking, as is Bernard Kelly's 'Passage Through Beauty' in *Blackfriars* Vol. XXXVI (September, 1935) pp 647–657. This last is a profound commentary on St. Thomas's dictum, 'Beauty is that which pleases when seen.' Finally, as if to demonstrate that Gill's thought is alive and flourishing the late E. F. Schumacher, in his *Good Work* (London, 1980), undertook a radical analysis of Western economic and industrial conditions and a forecast for the future on premises that might well have been intended as an extension and an application of Gill's thinking. This is not to claim that he goes beyond anything Gill conceived – he ignores, for instance, the question of the moral neutrality of capitalist investment, treats too superficially the question of what the worker

gets by working, does not make any real distinction between the tool and the machine, and has no metaphysics of
beauty – but his conclusions seem ample evidence that
Gill's doctrine could form a practical foundation to a re-
placement of the prevailing industrial system, one that will
hardly allow man survival into a *human* future.

I
First Things

1 It is no use, and no good, complaining about the world we live in and vaguely wanting something better, unless we are prepared to review the grounds of our life and its real meaning. CMA62

2 It is absolutely necessary to have principles, that is things that come first, the foundations of the house.

What we want to know is: what principles of common sense are relevant to the matter of human work. [. . .]

What principles are in harmony with divine revelation and in harmony with the conscience of man and the light of human reason? MM115

3 We have now to mount to higher planes and yet [. . .] we have to keep a firm and strong attachment to earth. While we attempt to grasp and to explain certain spiritual realities, we must not deny our bodily environment. WL108–9

4 We base ourselves upon the following affirmations: There is God. There is that which is not God – the spiritual and material creation, made by God out of nothing (nothing, strictly so called). This creation is a gratuity, and it is an expression of God's love for himself. AN291–2

5 In the beginning God created Heaven and Earth, and in the fullness of time – Man. God is a trinity of Persons: Father, Son and Spirit (these names indicate as nearly as words may, in the paucity of finite speech, the eternal relationship of the divine Persons; that the concatenation is hackneyed is no proof that it is without significance), and corresponding with the Three Persons of the Blessed Trinity are the

metaphysical categories, Truth, Goodness and Beauty, and all things are definable in terms of the Threefold Divinity who created them. Man therefore is to be defined in terms of the 'what', 'why' or 'how' of his existence.

The nature of man is likeness to God – for God created him in his image. He is a rational soul. The purpose of his existence is to know God, to serve God and to love God on earth and to be with him eternally in heaven. The manner of man's existence is incarnation. He is spirit and matter.

Man is, therefore, a creature capable of the knowledge, service and love of God. If he can know God he must have intelligence. If he can serve God he must have will. If he can love God he must have freedom. Nothing can love which is not free. The drawing together of things which are not free is properly called affection. Man is capable of love because he has free will. Freedom is not incompatible with discipline, it is only incompatible with irresponsibility.

The object of the intelligence is the true. The object of the will is the good. Therefore each of the two faculties, intellect and will, has its corresponding object. And freedom also has its proper object namely – love.

But though in thought these things are separable, in reality they are not so. Thus we cannot say of a thing: This is true but it is neither good nor lovely; we cannot say: This is good but it is neither true nor lovely; nor can we say: This is lovely but it is neither true nor good. In reality everything has a threefold significance, for everything combines in itself Truth, Goodness and Beauty, and everything may be defined by its intellectual content, by its moral content, or by its aesthetic content. The discovery of Truth is in answer to the question What (is it)? of Good to the question Why? and of Beauty to the question How? i.e. in what manner?

For as there are three persons in one God, so there are necessarily three qualities in every one thing: truth, goodness, beauty, and as the Holy Ghost proceeds from the

Father and the Son so beauty proceeds from truth and goodness. Beauty cannot exist by itself but proceeds from truth and goodness, as physical shape proceeds from Being and Purpose; and Love from Knowledge and Service. Beauty is not a quality in things independent of truth and goodness but is the exhibition of truth and goodness. It is perceived intuitively and the knowledge of it is developed by contemplation.   AN65–7

6 It is unquestionable that when God looked upon His works He saw that they were good; and the word 'good' implies appreciation of forms as well as ends. [. . .] my view is that in God's all-seeing mind He knew that Final and Formal like Righteousness and Peace would kiss one another (Psalm 84) [. . .] What I do jib at is the suggestion of a dichotomy; as though God could give roses five petals, or butterflies such and such pattern on their wings for any sort of separate reason, or vice versa that He could attend to the *structure* of things irrespective of *formal* results.   LT472

7 The unity of the human race must be taken for granted. Differences between one person and another or between one race and another and between the people of one time and another are simply differences of emphasis. This being so, it is to be expected that all human beings and all races will look to the same end, and all differences of achievement are to be attributed not so much to differences of aim as to differences of temper and circumstance. These facts are the more important when the subject of discussion is, as in the case of the arts, a thing of which the achievement has been so various. [. . .]

Now the end of the human race, the end to which all activity is directed is the discovery and grasping of the real. However variously this aim may be described or pursued; however erroneous may be the conclusions of reason; however distasteful may be the material achievements of one people to a people of another time or place; nevertheless Reality, what is real and not illusory, is what is sought by each and by all.   BLH208–9

8 God exists; He is a Person – the Personal Author and Ruler of all things. And *we are His people and the sheep of His pasture.* And we are made in His image – that is to say, we share in God's spiritual nature. We are rational beings and can deliberate and weigh the pros and cons of action; and having thus weighed, we can act freely. Whether or no we can do good of ourselves, we can certainly refrain from evil, even if we are to some extent – perhaps to a large extent – the victims of our physical and psychological *make-up.* We are, therefore, rightly held to be *responsible persons* and not automata obeying willy-nilly the forces to which we find ourselves subjected. And if we are thus children of God – for we are, in this religious view of man, more than just animals without responsibility (after all, you can punish a dog – but you cannot really *blame* him) – if we are children of God, then we are heirs also. We are called to some sort of sharing with God in His own life. We have what we call a *vocation.* We have, in fact, a destiny independent of our physical life on this earth. A destiny for which this physical life is a training ground and place of preparation [. . .] a place where we are *educated.*   LE41–2

9 Some philosophy, some religion, is behind all human works and is their primary instigation. Without some philosophy, some religion, nothing is done, nothing made, because nobody knows what to do or what to make, nobody knows what is good or what is bad. It has been said that the Church exists in order that words may have a meaning; it is also true that without philosophy and religion there is no meaning in human action.   AR20

10 In the end we find that there is only one being, and that we live only in him and by him.

Even so, truth is that which is knowable, and we know ourselves to be beings made for truth.

And the good is that which is desirable. Man is a being
which desires.

In seeking to know things, we reach out to them in order
to become one with them.

Prompted, provoked, moved, and stirred by desire, we
reach out to things in order to possess them.

Thus we desire what we know; and only what we know can
we desire.

The activity of desire we call will, and thus knowing and
willing are two movements of the soul, of man himself.

And the will is free.

Knowledge is not free – we can only know what is, and
there is no such thing as free thought – but willing implies choice, and in choosing we know ourselves to be
free.

We know ourselves to be responsible creatures. We know
ourselves to merit praise or blame. And we know these
things in the unquenchable light of nature.   CMA23

11   To the workman, the artist, the subject has always been all
in all. Unless he know what he is making he cannot make
anything. Whether it be a church or only a tooth-pick he
must know what it *is*; he must have it in his mind before he
can begin, before he can even choose his material or lay his
hand on a tool. And what a thing *is*, what things *are*, and,
inevitably, whether they are good or bad, worth making or
not, these questions bring him without fail to the necessity
of making philosophical and religious decisions. We may
accept the conclusions of others, it may, indeed, be better
that we should do so – provided 'we know in whom we
believe' – but conclusions must be accepted or the workman can make no beginning. So far from it being true that
religion and philosophy have no concern for the artist or he

for them, it is only when a religion and philosophy have become the unifying principle of a nation that any great works, whether steel bridges or stone shrines, are possible, and the decay of human art follows immediately upon the weakening of men's grasp upon the motives of action.   BLH226–7

12 It is not that I am saying that the works of men [. . .] are good because there is this or that philosophy and religion behind them. I am saying more than that. I am saying that it is because there is this or that philosophy and religion behind them that they are there at all – that it is to this or that philosophy and religion that such works owe their very existence, their very being.   AR16

13 It has been said*, and it is Catholic doctrine, that man is a bridge connecting the material and the spiritual. Both are real, both are good. God is spirit; man is matter and spirit. Man is therefore able to see, to present in material terms things spiritual and, conversely, though he cannot represent it, he is able to comprehend, though not fully, the spiritual significance of the material. He can show the spiritual in terms of matter, but he cannot show the material in terms of spirit.

The art of man, though ultimately unimportant, for, like all material things, works of art will return to dust, has therefore two claims to attention. In the first place, it is the only activity of which man is capable which is in itself worth pursuing and, in the second, it is man's sole abiding solace in this vale of tears.   AN232

14 Action is for the sake of contemplation, the active for the sake of the contemplative. To labour is to pray.

* Cf. Nietzsche: 'What is great in man is that he is a bridge and not a goal, a bridge leading from animal to beyond man.' But Nietzsche meant a sort of moving platform and taught no proper doctrine of the nature of man.

Work is the discipline (the yoga) by means of which 'body holds its noise and leaves Soul free a little.'

Recreation is for the sake of work. Leisure time is for the sake of recreation – in order that the labourer may the better return to work. Games are like sleep – necessary for the health of body and mind – a means to health, the health of the workman, the labourer, the man who prays, the contemplative. Leisure is secular, work is sacred. Holidays are the *active* life, the working life is the *contemplative* life.

The object of leisure is work. The object of work is holiness. Holiness means wholeness – it does not mean emaciate or emasculate. The holy man is the complete man – merry because 'he nothing lacks' – sad because of the sufferings, failures and penury of others. The holy man is the poor man; having nothing he possesses all things; the Kingdom of Heaven is within him.   ISL92

II

What is Man?

1 It is necessary to agree as to the nature of man for obvious
reasons. It is not possible, for any length of time, to keep
canaries in hen-coops or lions in monkey-houses. Unless
man's affairs are organized upon lines suitable to his nature
he must sooner or later react against the false system.

But, outside the Church, those who have not achieved
any agreement among themselves as to the nature of man
are fond of supposing, and proclaiming, that such agreement is impossible. They assume that man's nature is con-
stantly changing and that therefore a system suitable in one
age is unsuitable in another, that the changes in forms of
government and in conditions of work and employment
are as much measures of the changes in man's nature (the
thing they call 'progress') as they are indications of his
unrest and dissatisfaction under unsuitable conditions. In
answering such persons, we have not only got to satisfy
them as to the truth of our fundamental doctrine that man's
nature is now what it always has been – that man is man and
not brute, nor ever was – we have also got to answer the
question: why is it that, if man's nature is permanent and
definable, he does not appear ever to have achieved a
society as permanent as his nature? Why did not men, in the
beginning, agree to live according to their nature and refuse
to allow any change in their conditions?   AN6–7

2 What is human, what is man? Man is matter and spirit –
both real and both good. And what is this creature thus
compounded? He is a person. That is the point, the first
thing to be said, the first thing we know. And we know it
first from our own experience of ourselves and of our

fellow-men and women and not because we have been
taught it by scientific lecturers or read about it in books.
A person, a being who knows and wills and loves, who is
responsible for his acts and for the intended consequences
of his acts; a being who, because he is responsible, is able to
be damned, who merits praise or blame; a rational creature
knowing, by the light of his nature, true and false, good
and evil, right and wrong – not wholly or infallibly but
sufficiently – and, above all, a creature who loves – not
merely with the seeming obsequiousness of tame beasts
which scarcely know or will, but with the willing devotion
and self-sacrifice of beings who know in *whom* they believe.
That is briefly what we mean by the word person. It is no
philosophical invention, no abstraction, nothing which
either microscope or telescope could reveal; it is that which
we know ourselves to be.   ISL152–3

3 Man is matter and spirit and it is the spiritual which
  determines man in his species.   WL113

4 There is no before or after in spiritual matters. There is only
  being and non-being. If a spirit is, it is and there is no
  temporal or spatial beginning or end of it. You cannot say
  that the mind began with the body and ends with it. You
  can only say that the mind began to inform or determine or
  (figuratively) inhabit the body when the body began to be
  'habitable' or patient of determination or of being informed. The body has a temporal and spatial beginning and
  end, but not the mind. And that is why it may be said: I *have*
  a body, but not: I *am* a body. My body dies, but I am not my
  body; I have a brain, but what it does is not me though it is
  of me.
  [. . .]
    While the body lives it conditions mentality. The mind is
  not a product of the body, nor is it subject to it; it lives in it
  and is liable to be enthralled. The saying of Christ: 'Before

Abraham was, I am', is, as nearly as human words will allow, a statement of the non-temporal, non-spatial nature of personality; and another example is the reply received by Moses when he asked the name of God: 'I am who am'.   NB281–2

5 The ordinary man, 'the moral man' of the philosopher doesn't bother himself [. . .] with the abstruse difficulties of philosophical demonstration or proof; but he does not therefore throw away or reject or deny; on the contrary he affirms the common certainties of his experience. He knows himself for a person compounded of matter and spirit, and he looks to and yearns for personal immortality not as something fanciful [. . .] but as something obviously compatible with his compound nature. As the history of mankind shows, it is not belief in immortality that has been with difficulty instilled into him. The difficulty has been to get him to give it up. And the suggestion or the theory that such a belief has the nature of childish things to be put away with maturity has no foundation in fact for, as a child learns botany because it knows flowers, so men probe process because they know being.   NB286–7

6 There is a thing called Man and there is a thing called Nature
      – nature environs man.
   Is man one with his environment?
   Is he *precisely* one with it?
   That is the atheist affirmation.
   I have assumed that we deny it.
   It is in accord with all our experience to deny it.
   Walk about in a place removed from civilisation – some
      bare moorland, or polar ice cap.
   The common verdict of man is that in spite of his material
      harmony with his surroundings, his sharing in the life of
      birds and grasses, his dependence on air and warmth,

he also stands outside, above, beyond, independent and
aloof.

This proves nothing – but we are not here concerned with
proofs but with verdicts, with affirmation.

We affirm our nature, not by the faulty instruments of
induction and ratiocination, but by the convictions of
experience.

You know it is so.   SS32–3

7 Man, whatever his origins, is a creature who knows and
wills and loves, and if we find, up and down the world,
creatures who are undoubtedly men and yet who are cruel
and irresponsible and invincibly ignorant, we must assume
[. . .] that such barbarity is a degradation, or falling away from
nature. For to say that men are naturally barbarous is to
say that human beings are naturally *inhuman*, which is
absurd.   SS97

8 What is man? Man is matter and spirit, or, to give the word
spirit a more definite meaning, let us say, man is matter and
mind. And by the word *mind* we must understand both
intellect and will, and we must remember that those faculties are only separable in words; they are not separable in
actuality. The will cannot function without the intelligence
(you cannot will what you do not know), and the intelligence cannot function without the will (you cannot know
even the smallest thing without a prompting of the
will).   WP14

9 And man is a creature who loves.

Faith is knowledge; by faith we know.

Hope and desire are fellows; we do not desire without
hope or hope without desire. We do not will without hope
or hope against our wills.

Faith, hope and love – these three; but the greatest of
these is love.

By knowledge we possess things;

By will we reach out to them;

By love we draw them to ourselves that we may be possessed by them.

But perhaps we must distinguish here. The natural and instinctive attraction we feel towards things, whether of sight or sound, touch or taste or smell, is good; for these things are in themselves good, and to possess them, in due order, is necessary to a normal life.   CMA24–5

10 It is man's special gift to know holiness.   MM101

11 Holiness is moral integrity become an art, a thing admirable in itself, a thing made. Holiness like art is more than prudence, it is prudence become an end instead of remaining simply a means. Such is the holiness of the saints and there is always a certain gaiety about it, the gaiety of men set free.   ACC132

12 All men have a nose for holiness. [. . .]

    Holiness is the test – but you must train your noses. You must train yourselves to know the smell of Paradise. MM102–3

13 As Edward Johnston used to insist: 'Man is the consciousness of God' – that was the primary truth – i.e. that the universe arrived at consciousness by arriving at man, and the universe being a creation and therefore manifestation of God, the primary act of consciousness was consciousness of God. God was conscious in the universe by means of man, who, as it were, bounced the ball back to him.   AU165

14 Therefore God is the only enjoyable being. [. . .] the author and source of all enjoyment.

    And as God is the source of all enjoyment, to enjoy oneself is, actually, to share God's enjoyment. When it says: 'I have said you are Gods', and when it says: 'God created

man to his own image' (Psalm 81, 6; Genesis 1, 27), it means
what it says – that we are 'sons of the most High' and 'if
sons, heirs also'. Therefore when the child says: I am enjoying myself eating this lovely apple, it really means: God and
I are enjoying ourselves – I am enjoying myself in Him
and He through me. And when the child says this apple is
lovely, it really means: I see this apple in God.   WL111–3

15 The truth remains: man is matter and spirit – both real and
both good, and escape is impossible. Salvation, the salvation of men, and that is to say the wholeness, and that again
is to say the *holiness* of men, is not attainable by denying
either side or component of his nature. The only question
is: Which shall rule? And to this question there can be only
one answer. Man is matter and spirit, but the primacy is of
the spirit. [. . .] The primacy of the spirit is a fact of our
experience. We know ourselves as persons and therefore as
governed, ruled, ordered, and led (however often we have
been or are misled) by our personal selves. We may and
must allow its due weight to the physical and material
world which conditions our lives, and all its geological,
geographical, climatic, racial and economic forces and
circumstances; but those things did not make us; they are
simply the conditions under and in which we live. We
neglect or deny them at our peril; but to deny our spiritual
nature and its primacy is not merely dangerous, it is man's
damnation. The integrity of the individual means exactly
that – the realization of man's dual nature and the primacy
of the spirit.   ISL154–5

III

The Four Causes

1 There are four causes for the existence of anything. And this fact, though it wears the garb of philosophy, is a matter of common sense and of uncommon importance. [. . .] the four causes are as follow: the Final cause, the Efficient cause, the Material cause and the Formal cause.

[. . .]

But let us take the causes one by one. Take a saw and cut down a tree and keep the stump. You have now got a tree stump of a certain kind, and not only have you a stump of a certain kind but you have a particular stump, an individual one – this kind and not that kind, this particular one and not that, a stump like this one and not like that one. What makes a tree stump a tree stump, and what makes this particular stump this particular shape is the Formal Cause, and without that cause this particular stump would not exist. The Formal Cause is that which determines a thing in its essence. What is it? That is its formality. [. . .]

But a formality cannot exist by itself. What further is necessary? Here is this tree stump. It is made of wood. If there were not this wood this stump would not exist. My power to use a saw would be of no avail if there were no material to use it on. Even that kind of a sculptor who, waking from a kind of trance, finds his imagination seething with ideas or images, cannot imagine things made of nothing, and, even if he be indifferent as to what material he uses, he cannot use none. And whatever stuff he chooses will cause a particular result. The material of which things are made is called a 'cause' of their existence, because a thing existing in this material rather than that differs from another thing existing in a different material, and one cause of the difference between this thing and that thing is the difference of material. Therefore the material is said to be a 'cause' of that difference and, inasmuch as a material thing exists in such and such a manner and not otherwise, the material may be said to be one cause of its existence.

But, given the material, there is not therefore a thing made. There must also be an effective principle. In human makings there is first of all the will to act, but the human will is only effective by means of other existing things. Suppose you have the will to play a game of football. Suppose there is a ball and a football field. But unless there be a foot there will be nothing doing. And the foot must be moved. The will effects the movement of the ball by means of the foot. This is the Efficient Cause. There is no difficulty about this. Efficiency is obviously a cause of the existence of things, and if there were no effective power to move material, human things would have to remain unmade.

But even now – here is this tree stump, made of wood, cut with a saw, but why? What is it *for*? By reason of its actual, real form, it is this tree stump and not another. We know what it *is*, but not *why*. To what *end* was the tree stump sawn and shaped? Was it made to sit on, or what? What moves the will to act?

Suppose I say to myself: I will make something. Here are forests and mountains, metals and muscles, making something seems called for. But I have no idea what! My mind is a blank – or it is filled with reflected images like the back-plate of a camera, but I see nothing to be made, nothing as I might make it. Here is a tree [. . .], but I see nothing in it, it means nothing to me, I have no wooden images in my mind, therefore no will to make one. My muscles are as useless as this wood, and all the tools and machinery you can give me are wasted.

Or suppose my mind is seething with ideas but that I have no adequate reason for making anything. The flattery of rich connoisseurs does not seem adequate. The placing of things in museums seems absurd. The mere exhibition of my own idiosyncrasy, even if the exhibition be well paid, seems a foolish proceeding. [. . .]

Or suppose I 'go abstract' and become enthralled in what, according to the jargon of 'art' critics, is called 'the relations of masses'. Suppose I have a sort of mystical aesthetic trances and my works are hailed as 'revelations of the reality underlying appearances'. What then? Are such things a proper object for the bargainings of 'art' dealers, and are the boudoirs and 'art' galleries of London and Paris and Berlin and New York the proper temples for the worship of reality? And do I not know that, however much I may flatter myself that my own motives are pure and my inspiration genuine, the only real result of this 'high art' connoisseur business is the flattery of a more or less decadent rich class and the 'boosting' of their decadent 'values'? Would I not rather make something really useful to ordinary human beings?

Or suppose I am an ordinary carpenter and my mind is filled with ideas for cupboards and tables. But who wants tables and cupboards, and why? And the people who want them and the reasons they want them for must necessarily determine the sort of things they get or are given. If, like the rich connoisseurs of 'high art', the people who buy ordinary furniture are filled with foolish ideas and all sorts of snobbery, so that the furniture dealers and their wage slaves, the carpenters, are more concerned to exploit their customers' foolishness than to give them good things (whatever good things may be), then shall I, an ordinary carpenter, have any really adequate reason for making cupboards and tables? And is the fact that I earn my living by so doing an adequate reason for working if I have no adequate reason for living, no end in view, no final cause of my life itself?

What moves the human will? This is the Final Cause. And though for the real existence of anything all four causes are equally necessary, and from the point of view of being and non-being it is impossible to leave out any, from the point of view of the spirit of man, his mind, the ruling partner in his duality of matter and spirit, from the point of view of all those things existing in what Marx calls 'the ideological spheres', the final cause is more important than all the other three. What you make, what you make it of, how you do it are all comparatively unimportant when compared with why you make it, your reason for action. The final cause is the first cause, and the end is the beginning.

But here it must be pointed out that this classification of causes will cause as much confusion as clarity if it be forgotten that the classification is mainly for convenience. There is no real separation of one cause from the others. In any existing thing its final cause co-exists with its formal cause, the formal co-exists with the material, and all three depend upon and are of no effect without the efficient cause. You cannot imagine a thing made of nothing or made without reason or purpose; and you cannot imagine a thing made 'no how'. [. . .] Nevertheless the classification is important and useful, for it helps us to see our acts in proportion and perspective.

And, above all, the classification of causes is important because it helps us to restore and maintain ourselves in our integrity. Man is not a brute beast, subject to God's law (or, if you prefer, the 'law of Nature') but not giving any knowing, willing and loving response; he is a responsible creature, an instrument of creation, an instrument by means of which that is made which cannot be made otherwise. Responsibility does not only imply a burden imposed; it also implies a power to bring gifts. It is his power of willing response that gives to man his unique responsibility. And that response is primarily of the mind. Therefore it is that our industrialism, as such, is to be condemned; for it reduces the workman to a 'subhuman condition of intellectual irresponsibility'.   NB316–23

IV
What is Art?

1 The Incarnation may be said to have for Its object the drawing of men from misery to happiness. Being the act of God It is the greatest of all rhetorical acts and therefore the greatest of all works of art. And as from the fatherhood of God all paternity is named in heaven and earth, so from His creative power all art is named. In the Incarnation we do not only know a fact of history or a truth of religion; we behold a work of art, a thing *made*. As a fact of history It is the most interesting and illuminating of all historical happenings. As a truth of religion It is of primary and fundamental importance. But it is as a work of art that It has saving power, power to persuade, power to heal, power to rescue, power to redeem.   LE9

2 God's work of creation was gratuitous. Man also is able to make gratuitously. He is able to make things simply because it pleases him so to do, and things such that they are simply pleasing to him. Such things are works of art pure and simple. They leave the world better than they found it, but that is not their raison d'être; their reason of being is the pleasure pure and undiluted of the rational being who made them. They do not set out to serve him; they add to his physical well-being only by accident.   AN293

3 The word 'art' first of all meant skill, and it still means that first of all. And it means human skill, the skilful doing which results in making, so that, in its full meaning, the word 'art' meant, and still means, the power in the mind of man so to direct his acts that the result of his thought and actions is a thing made. But though that is the original meaning of the word, and though that meaning is still the true one, we have

nowadays almost completely forgotten it, and have come to
think of art as though the word did not mean all human
works whatsoever, from drain-pipes to cathedrals, from
paper-weights to statues of saints or politicians, from street
cries to songs and symphonies, from sign-boards to Royal
Academy paintings, but only the special works of the
special people who paint pictures, carve or mould statues,
write books and poems, and design buildings to be looked
at.

'The artist is not a special kind of man, but every man is a
special kind of artist.'* This is a true saying; but we no longer
believe it.   CMA28–9

4 The artist earns his living by doing what [. . .] it is his
vocation to do – he acts according to his nature (Aristotelian
sense of the word), not according to his whim.   LT363

5 The word skilful does not merely mean well done, it means
well made. And when we say a person does his work 'skil-
fully' we mean that his very action is a thing to be seen, a
thing which we can admire in itself, a work of art, a
thing made. And we momentarily forget the purpose of his
action, though only momentarily; otherwise, however skilful, the action would be meaningless and, being meaningless, would cease to be a human act. For human acts are all
rational acts. They are acts determined by mind – by intelligence and will (though there is not of course any necessary
process of ratiocination about them. Many acts are done
without a process of reasoning; but they are not therefore unreasonable, irrational). And that is why, as the
philosopher says, 'Art abides entirely on the side of the
mind'.† Art is skill, skill in making, human skill, the skill of
rational beings.   WL14–5

* Ananda K. Coomaraswamy, *The Transformation of Nature in Art*, (Harvard,
   (1935) p. 64.
† See Jacques Maritain, *Art and Scholasticism*, translated by J. F. Scanlan, (1930)
   chapter 4:3.

6 Art abides entirely on the side of the mind. Yes, and the
   idea of a drain-pipe must be as clearly in the mind as the
   idea of a painting. There is no escape from mental responsibility. But the word art means skill: neither the painting nor
   the drain-pipe would exist, either as pleasing objects or as
   useful ones, without the skill of their makers. All sorts of
   people have fine ideas, all sorts of people wish to serve their
   fellow-men by supplying them with things which please
   them or minister to their physical convenience, every man
   is potentially what is called an artist, but the fact remains,
   the artist is the person who actually has the skill and actually
   uses his skill to make things, to make, to bring into physical
   existence the things which abide in his mind. An artist is
   not simply a person with ideas. He is a person who has the
   skill to make his ideas manifest. He is not even a person
   with fine ideas or even fine skill; such a person is simply a
   better artist than others. Art itself is neither good nor bad;
   there is every kind of art, from the silliest and most inept to
   that which embodies the most refined sensibility in the
   most perfectly precise form.   ACC4–5

7 So all things made are works of art and, of art, skill is the *sine
   qua non*. There are different arts and therefore different kinds
   of skill. [. . .] There are two main divisions of art work – the
   arts whose business is to make things which affect other
   things and those whose business it is to affect persons, the
   one to affect the movement of matter (as all tools and
   machines and objects of physical utility) the other to affect
   the motions of the mind (as all paintings and sculptures and
   music and poetry) – would it not be better [then] to reserve
   the name of art definitely for one kind or the other and find
   or invent another name for the one not to be called art?
   Thus, in deference to the writers on painting and sculpture,
   the persons commonly called 'art' critics, we might reserve
   the name art for all those arts whose sole business it is to

affect the mind and we might call all the other manufactures something else.

What is the objection to this? There are two insuperable objections. First of all the just use of common speech forbids it. The word art does indeed mean skill. We cannot forbid such phrases as the art of cooking or the art of the pickpocket. We cannot deny that artful means 'full of some kind of skill', that the artificer is some kind of skilful man and that the word artificial simply means 'made by the deliberate skill of men,' rather than by the instinctive operations of animals or the impersonal force of inorganic nature, and does not necessarily imply anything to do with those works whose object is to make manifest the ideas and imaginations of painters and sculptors, musicians and poets.

The second objection is even more overwhelming. It is this: that there is in fact no hard and fast division and separation between the two kinds of art. It is not normal to men to make even machines without paying some attention to the fact that machines are seen and heard and touched as well as used. Even though the designer of airplane engines thinks very little of the appearance of his mechanism, it is obvious that this thoughtlessness is not characteristic of the designer of locomotives, still less of the designer of carts and carriages, of fountain-pens and foot-warmers, of fire-escapes and frying-pans. All these persons, these artists, [. . .] are concerned for the appearance of the things they make.* Still more obvious is this in the case of the building and furnishing arts. Who can deny that building is an art which touches at every point both the sphere of physical utility and the sphere of the affections?   ACC9–11

8 [But it may be said,] 'What we object to is the notion that art

---

*i.e. they realize that the things they make are also objects to be contemplated as beings and not merely as instruments.

is skill and that material finish or precision has anything to
do with it.'

The confusion of mind here is a confusion between the
notions of doing and making and a confusion between
doing deeds and making things. Art is skill; but it is skill in
making. It is not mere dexterity; it is dexterity directed
towards making. The business of the pickpocket is called an
art when we regard the business not simply as that of
extracting coins from pockets unbeknown, but when we
regard the pickpocket as making a nice job of it – when we
can see the act as a thing made. The act of the artist is not a
prudential act. It is an act directed to the good of the thing
to be made.

Skill in making, the thing called art, degenerates into
mere dexterity, i.e. skill in doing, when the workman, for
whatever reason [. . .] ceases to be concerned for the thing
made or, having become a mere tool, a 'hand' in the
employ of another, has no longer any responsibility for the
thing made and has therefore lost the knowledge of what it
is that he is making. [. . .] In many factories the 'hands'
cannot even know what they are *supposed* to be making. All
their acts are deeds. All their acts are prudential acts. They
polish this or twist the other simply because they are told to
do so. They obey because their wage depends on it and
they depend on their wage. The factory hand can only
know what he is *doing*. What is being made is no concern of
his.

[. . .] Art is skill in making; but the thing to be made must
first of all be known in the mind. If it be not known in the
mind it is obvious that no degree of surface finish or jug-
gling with tools will bring it into existence. The trouble in
those times and places where technical dexterity takes the
place of skill in making is not at all in the fact of technical
dexterity, for dexterity is in itself good. The trouble is
simply the degradation of the mind. In such times and

places the artist, the responsible workman is without clear ideas and without desire. He does not know what he is making; he does not see it clearly in his mind or he does not desire above all things to make it. [. . .]

Art is skill in making; the good work is the skilful work, the work in which the appropriate means have been employed to effect the desired end. If inappropriate means have been employed, the end will not, cannot be achieved. Everything depends upon the nature of the end desired and ends are many and various. It is obvious that the workman must know what he wants to make before he begins the work; it is equally obvious that he must be able to make it or the thing will not be made. Knowing what is to be made is one thing, and knowledge is a thing which may be acquired by anyone; it is connatural to man to know what he desires and all men in consequence are potentially artists; but the word art means skill in making and the name of artist is reserved to him who has the skill to make things and does actually make them.   ACC22–4

9 The relation between the image in the mind of the maker and the executed work is one of more or less complete identity – more complete in the case of physically useful things, less complete in that of objects whose usefulness is spiritual. The reason of this is that the final cause, the end of the work, in the case of the physically useful object is more defined and, being defined, its limits are easily recognised and can be perceived by one sweep of the mind. But in the case of paintings, sculptures, music and poetry the limits being spiritual are less easily discernible.   ACC15

10 The most important motives for man's activity in doing or making are neither animal instincts nor caprice. We hold that love is more important and not merely prettier than instinct. Upon such a ground and from such a place of vantage we survey the works of men. We see all things as

evidence of love. We make what we love – in accordance with our loves so we make. A pair of scissors, no less than a cathedral or a symphony, is evidence of what we hold good, and therefore lovely, and owes its being to love.   AR17

11 Man is a being, an entity. He is not merely an instrument, a tool, a 'hand'. And the things he makes should properly reflect his nature – not merely his idiosyncrasy, the thing art critics call 'self-expression' – his nature as a creature that knows and wills and loves and, above all things, loves. And further, the things men make do not properly exhibit man's nature as a lover unless they are orientated towards the proper object of his love. It is not necessary that there should be any shy-making talk about working for the Glory of God. But it is very necessary, it is entirely necessary that it should be possible to say of men's work that it does in fact give God glory, that the work of man is that kind of work. It is not necessary to talk about it; but it is necessary that it should be so. It is not desirable that everybody should always be talking about love; but it is absolutely necessary that, if man's work is to be a proper and normal expression and exhibition and product of his real nature, every work of man should have the nature of a love song.   WL120–1

12 This worship of God which a man displays in his work we call Beauty. Beauty is not to be confused with loveliness. Beauty is absolute, loveliness is relative. It is for the love of God and his worship that a man deals justly by the work of his hands. Beauty is not an accidental perfection either of God's creation or of man's handiwork. Beauty is an Essential Perfection of Creation and of handiwork. Beauty is the Love of God sensible in his work. Beauty is the Love of God and his praise and worship sensible in the work of man's hands.   AN3–4

13 To say, therefore, that philosophy and religion are the effec-
    tive motive in human works, works of love no less than
    works of power, of beauty no less than of usefulness, is
    simply to say that God is the instigator of all good works,
    and that the good workman is the man of God, and this is,
    in an especial manner, true in respect of those works
    whereof beauty is the formal cause. 'After God all paternity
    in heaven and earth is named,' (Ephesians III:15) and this
    does most precisely mean that all creative acts have God for
    their author. The human act of begetting is a type of divine
    creative power. The act of the artist in the creative imagin-
    ation is, as the schoolmen pointed out, the nearest human
    counterpart.* And, though it be true that his imagination is
    nourished and sustained by vision and hearing and all the
    senses, because and in so far as the idea of the artist is not
    formed by what he sees but is formative of what he makes,
    so and so far is he actually a creator – the father indeed of
    his works.   BLH249–50

14 More particularly is art the peculiar and appropriate occu-
    pation of men when men are consciously devoted to the
    service and love of God. Then indeed no other manner of
    occupation will seem worthy. Those men who give them-
    selves entirely to contemplation, who would seem there-
    fore least to merit the name of artist, are in fact the most
    completely artists, for not only are they artificers in the
    shaping of their own souls, but they are, God guiding,

---

* ['"Art imitates Nature in her manner of operation" (St. Thomas). In other
words, as every traditional treatise on metaphysics or theology con-
tinually asserts, the human artificer works like the Divine Artificer, with
only this important distinction, that the human artificer has to make use
of already existing materials, and to impose new forms on these
materials, while the Divine Artificer provides his own material out of the
infinitely "possible" which is not yet, and is therefore called "nothing",
whence the expression *ex nihilo fit*.' A. K. Coomaraswamy, op. cit, Vol. 1
p. 54.]

artificers in the shaping of life itself. The religious life is man's greatest work of art. It is a comparatively simple matter to shape a stone to one's liking, but the devils themselves conspire to hinder man's efforts to shape his own life. Therefore, though not every man is called to the life of 'religion', every man is called to the love of God and every man is called to give love to the work of his hands. Every man is called to be an artist.

But just as the good religious prays without noticing that he is praying, so the good workman works without noticing that he is an artist. Self-consciousness is not essential; indeed it is a hindrance. Self-forgetfulness, self-abnegation is the proper state of mind for man. Thus, and thus alone, can he collaborate with God in creating.   AN197–8

15   *'The invisible things of God may be clearly seen, being understood by the things which are made.'* (Romans 1:20)

The word was made flesh; that is to say: 'the day-spring from on high has visited us', and in our works we reach nearest to that highness when, in a manner of speaking, we carry on that visitation. But we are not to suppose that because pictures and sculptures and poetry are or may be more explicitly rhetorical than chairs and tables that there is or need be any greater holiness in works of fine art than in other works. We know God by sight in the person of Our Lord, but we know Him by sight in and through *all* His works. When God looked at the world of His creation 'He saw that it was good'. But 'one alone is good', God Himself. Therefore God sees Himself reflected in His creation and we also may see Him thus. His creation is not Himself but it is His word, not *the* Word but *His* word, a word that we may hear.

    . . . *emittit eloquium suum terrae;*
    *velociter currit sermo ejus.**

---

* ['(Who) sendeth forth his speech to the earth;/ his word runneth swiftly.'
Psalm 147:15]

Thus again we are confronted by a rhetorical activity. In His creation God invites our attention, draws us to Him, craves our love. And we may carry on the same work; we may collaborate with Him in creating.   LE13

16 When a person says: 'I don't know anything about art, but I know what I like', he is making a perfectly just remark.

What he likes: that is to say, what pleases him.

We only ask, just as we demand it of artists, the he take some trouble to exercise his mind – his apparatus for liking – that he keep his mind in good training.

'A good life is a mortified life.'

Good taste is mortified taste.

Mortified – that is, taste in which the stupid, the sentimental, the irrelevant is killed.*   BLH193

---

*['The individual who has been rightly educated should not "know what he likes" only, but "like what he knows." The man who asserts "I do not know anything about art, but I know what I like" is governed by sensual appetite in the same sense as is he who says "I do not know what I think, but I know what I like thinking," or "I do not know what is right, but I know what I like doing".' Coomaraswamy, op. cit, Vol 1, p. 81.]

V

Art and Prudence

1 Art! What is art but simply skill? That is the root meaning of the word and no tree can afford to do without its root. The root is the thing which attaches it to the earth – through which it draws material nourishment, elemental nourishment. [. . .] So it is with art – it is rooted in the earth and its roots are the skill of men. [. . .] The skill, then, which is the root of art is a man's skill – man, a creature having free will, a rational soul, a creature made to know, love and serve God and to do these things of his own free will. Art is therefore *deliberate* skill. And bad art is not therefore unskilful – it is simply skill contaminated, deprived of its proper object by foolishness or ill will.

So, if skill is the root of art, its trunk is deliberation. Art, as a notable French philosopher [Maritain] said – echoing, as I understand, the schoolmen of old – 'art abides entirely on the side of the mind' – a work of art is a thing which a man has made deliberately as well as he can and as well as he knows how – even bad art is that. [. . .] But here we must remember that a work of art is a *thing* – it is a thing *made* – it is not a deed *done*. A work of art is not an act of prudence. Prudence, even worldly prudence, is not concerned with things but with deeds – deeds having relation to an end in view whether it be the obtaining of worldly advantage simply or that last end – the Beatific Vision. But art is concerned with the thing, not the man – it is concerned with the end of the work.   AN257–8

2 Skill in making and skill in doing are both loosely called art. Doing is an activity directed to an end in view – the end in view being man's good, his last good, Heaven.

But when a man's deeds are directed not to his own good
    simply but to the good of a *thing*, then doing becomes
    making.

An act that is good, or thought to be good, with regard to
    oneself is called a *prudent* act.

An act that is good, or thought to be good, with regard to a
    thing to be made is called *art*.

A man whose acts are conformed to his own good is called
    a *prudent man*.

A man whose acts are conformed to the good of things is
    called an *artist*.

  In both cases skill in doing is required.

  Skill in doing good to oneself is called *prudence*.

  Skill in doing good to things is called *art*.

Prudence is the means to happiness in oneself.

Art is the means to pleasure in what is not oneself.

  To have happiness is the object of prudence.

[. . .]

Ethics is the science of happiness in oneself.

Aesthetics is the science of pleasure in things.

  Both are departments of philosophy.

Prudence is the application of ethics to practice.

Art is the application of aesthetics to practice.

  The practice of prudence is called morals.

  The practice of art is called craft or craftsmanship.

[. . .]

Now the perfectly prudent man is a man of perfectly good
    will.

The perfect artist is a man of perfectly good sense.

Perfectly good will is, it seems, possible to man.

Perfectly good sense is, it seems, not possible to man.

  His finite condition deprives him of the possibility of
    perfect knowledge.

Moreover, the perfection of good will is passive: –

  'Grant that I may love thee always: then do with me what

thou wilt,' and again: 'Be it done to me according to thy word.'

But perfect good sense is active:

(The words of God effect what they signify.)

Man can be perfectly passive.

Man cannot be perfectly active.

He can do nothing of himself.

'We are not able to please thee by our own acts.'

Man can only be a perfectly willing agent.

His free will does not give him creative power.

It gives him simply perfect power to will what God wills.

A finite intelligence does not give him perfect knowledge of what God knows.

Hence prudence is superior to art with regard to man, but 'art . . . metaphysically is superior to prudence.'*

BLH12–9

3 As the created universe is primarily a work of art and not primarily a work of kindness (that is why praise comes before thanksgiving and art is metaphysically above prudence), so works of art are more essentially human than works of usefulness or even than works of kindness (hence the 'Humanities' does not mean Ethics but Arts).　BLH76

4 The prudent man acts so that he may achieve the blissful state of heavenly happiness.

But that state is one in which he has knowledge of all things in God – *Gaudium de veritate*.

Happiness is therefore not separable from pleasure in things.

Prudence is therefore not separable from art.

As making has need of doing – so prudence has need of art.

The achieving of happiness in oneself is the business of prudence.

The supplying of pleasure in things is the business of art.

* Maritain, op. cit, p. 84.

Art and prudence are, as it were, one flesh.
>   There is a marriage between them.
>   There is also a lovers' quarrel between them.
>   Each seeks the perfection of its own.   BLH15–6

5   The lovers' quarrel between art and prudence has become an unloving 'scrap'.
The opposition has become a conflict.
The man of prudence is shocked by the artist's inclination
>   to value things as ends in themselves –
>   Worth *making* for their own sakes –
>   Loved for their beauty.
He sees *idolatry* at the end of that road.
He is also shocked by the artist's acceptance of all things of sense
>   as beautiful and therefore pleasing in themselves –
>   Worth *having* for their own sakes –
>   Loved for their pleasantness.
He sees sensuality at the end of that road.
Upon the other hand, the artist is shocked by the prudent man's inclination to see things merely as means to ends –
>   Not worth anything for their own sakes –
>   Their beauty neither seen nor loved.
He sees Manchester at the end of that road.
He is also shocked by the prudent man's inclination to see in the pleasures of sense mere filthiness.
>   To him that is a kind of blasphemy.
The prudent man accuses the artist of sin.
The artist cries 'blasphemer' in reply.
>   They see no good in one another.   BLH23–4

6 Let us return to the beginning.
Prudence is concerned with the man.
Art is concerned with the thing.
Man is more important than things.

Prudence is more important than art.

Man's end is happiness.

The end of art is pleasure.

But happiness consists in pleasure.

> Happiness is the state of being *pleased* with things, of being pleased with *things*.

Making pleasing things is the business of art.

The pleasure of the senses is good.

Art which aims at pleasing the mind through the senses is good.

The pleasure of the mind is good.

Art which aims at pleasing the mind and in regard to which the senses are disinterested is good.

But man is matter and spirit –

> Both are real and both good.

An art which pleases the senses only and does not make its appeal to the whole man is necessarily bad art.

An art which makes its appeal to the mind only and does not please the whole man is necessarily bad art.

That is good art which pleases the senses as they ought to be pleased and the mind as it ought to be pleased.

With good art prudence should have no quarrel.   BLH26–8

7 St. Augustine said: 'Love God and do what you will.'

> *Dilige Deum et fac quod vis.*

The artist says: 'Love and make what you like.'

> This is the highest prudence.

> But the prudent man thinks them dangerous sayings: for though most men know what they like doing or making, few men know certainly that they love God.

> Nevertheless, these rules are the only really safe rules.

It is the business of the prudent man to inculcate the love of God.

The love of God involves acceptance of what God has revealed and obedience to His law.

But 'the service of God is perfect freedom.'
This is not because love makes the law of no effect but because he who loves God loves what God loves.

BLH21

VI
Of Beauty

1 'The beauty of God,' says St. Thomas Aquinas, quoting Denis [St. Dionysios], 'is the cause of the being of all that is.'*
BLH25

2 The beautiful thing is that which being seen pleases (*Id quod visum placet*).† This is an obvious fact. It is neither a definition of beauty nor of beautifulness, it is simply a statement of fact. [. . .] The only difficulty is with regard to the meaning attached to the words 'seen' and 'pleases'.   ACC127

3 It is only in respect of beauty that man is a creator. The search for truth is not invention; it is the search for what is. All good deeds are but means to ends; they are not ends in themselves. Only the beautiful is an end in itself and only beauty is ever new. That which is beautiful pleases when seen, and it is the mind which sees and is pleased. The mind, compounded of intellect and will, sees and is pleased by the beautiful – the beautiful compounded of the true and the good. But there is no need for the good workman to talk about it or even be able to do so, and as the good man prays without knowing that he is praying, so the good workman may work well without knowing that he is wise or remembering that God exists.   BLH250

4 Knowledge of the beautiful is of this nature, and it is by what we call common sense that men appreciate what is in accordance with right conduct, that is to say with Prudence, that is to say with 'man's last end', that is to say with man's destiny as child of God and inheritor of the

* St. Thomas Aquinas, *de Divinis Nominibus*, Lecture 5.
† St. Thomas, *Summa Theologica*, I, Q5 and 4.

Kingdom of Heaven, so it is by a *common sensibility*, as I may now call it, that men appreciate what is in accordance with right making, that is to say with art, that is to say with the nature of things as manifesting the creative love of God, that is to say Beauty itself. [. . .] It is without doubt that as all goodness in men is a reflection of the goodness of God and an earnest of man's godward direction, so all beauty is a reflection of the divine beauty, and [. . .] man's pleasure in things seen or heard is in fact only understandable when explained as a pleasure in what is in accordance with reality, pure Being, God Himself.   BLH233–4

5 'The mind acts, and its very act is, absolutely speaking, life *par excellence*; but it is an *immanent* act . . . by which, with boundless voracity, it takes hold on Being, and draws it to itself, eats and drinks it, so as to become itself, in a certain manner, all things.'* In its nature this first leap is not an act of discursive reasoning. It is not made by a process of ratiocination. Its nature is aesthetic. For if man has been, from the beginning, a tool-using animal, a workman depending upon his reasonable intelligence, he has also, from the beginning, been enamoured of beauty, a contemplative for whom nothing was merely a means to an end, but for whom all things were delectable as ends in themselves.

'Beauty', as the scholastics observed, is a 'lightening of intelligence over matter intelligently arranged',† and man's avidity for beauty is more significant than any of his other appetites. He apprehends beauty immediately, and therefore apprehends Being. This apprehension is a short cut. It transcends reason, by it man reaches certainty without need or desire of proof. 'It is for her beauty that wisdom is beloved' 'I am fallen in love with her beauty', as it says in the Book of Wisdom. And, I may add, it is through, or by means

* Maritain, *Art and Scholasticism*, p. 3.
† Maritain, op cit, p. 25.

of her beauty that wisdom, the knowledge of things in their ultimate causes, is known first of all to men. [. . .] It is to be regarded as a leap of beings capable of *seeing* the truth.
[. . .]
This leap of the mind, the mind uniting the powers of intellect and will, is a leap of the whole man. It is an act of love, a fling of the heart as well as a movement of the understanding, and this movement is prerequisite 'not only to the experiences of the beautiful as such, but to any knowledge of the real that is not merely information'.*   NB53–5

6 Beauty – the word is a stumbling block.
      Do not let us stumble over it.
      Beauty is the *Splendour of Being*. The primary constituent of visible Being is Order.
      Beauty [. . .] is conspicuous order – order shining out. Hence it is of the mind. It is the mind that is pleased by things called beautiful. (The kinds of pleasure which are not primarily of the mind are generally called *lovely*, because lovable, i.e. desired and desirable, satisfying a physical need or appetite rather than a mental.)
But the lovely and the beautiful are mixed – because man is matter as well as mind [. . .]
Hence man's work is concerned with both the *beautiful* and the *lovely*.
But art is specifically concerned with the beautiful – that is its ratio – its *raison d'etre* – its reason of being.
Beauty – conspicuous order.
The Beautiful – conspicuous order in things.
Order – rightly ruled, governed, arranged, proportioned.
Rightly – in accordance with the demands of mind.
Mind – *intellect*, i.e. the faculty of knowing, and *will* – i.e. the faculty of reaching out to things, grasping them, acting, ordering, governing in accordance with what is known.

* Bernard Kelly, 'Passage Through Beauty', in *Blackfriars*, Sept. 1935, pp. 647–57.

When a thing is well made, well ordered, the mind of him
  who contemplates it is at rest, is satisfied – is pleased.
This pleasure is not of the senses – though the senses share it
    Nor is it the pleasure of knowing.
    It is not simply that kind of pleasure which we have
when we discover the right solution of a problem.
    Nor is it simply that kind of pleasure which we have
when we see or receive an act of kindness.
It is the delight of the mind in seeing the thing itself.
    It follows immediately upon the mind's grasping or
comprehension of the thing presented to it.
    It is the result of the mind's recognition of what is after
its own kind.
    In things of beauty the mind comes into its own.
    BLH66–8

7 The beautiful thing is that which, being seen, pleases, and it
is man that is pleased. Man is matter and spirit. Things are
therefore pleasing to him according to two modes. First, he
may be pleased sensually, as when he is pleased by a
physical sensation, a sensation of physical well being, or
one which he delights in as such even though experience
may go to show that it is physically harmful and leads
towards ill health and death. Such pleasure is not the term
of a process of reasoning, though it may be enhanced when
reason judges it to be in harmony with reason – prudence,
the good of man, his last end. But though sensual pleasure
is not the term of a process of reasoning it is not therefore
unreasonable; it is not therefore an inhuman thing. It is the
man, body and mind, who enjoys, and not merely his body.
    Secondly, he may be pleased mentally, as when he is
pleased by things which, though they produce no consciously experienced bodily sensation, seem to him to be
holy; that is right and good, whole, not deprived of anything properly due to them; things in harmony with the

good which is the object of his will and with the truth, the reality which is the object of his intelligence. Truth is the conformity of the mind with things. Good is the conformity of the mind with the purpose of things. And beauty is the conformity of mind with things and their purpose – not Apollo, not Dionysos, but Apollo and Dionysos. But though mental pleasure is not accompanied, necessarily or in our experience, by bodily sensation, it is not therefore an inhuman thing. It is the man who is illumined by the illumination of beauty – the man, body and soul. For it is by means of objects of sense that he knows, and the fact is that things are not so much known in themselves as that they are means to knowledge.

Therefore, just as what we call sensual pleasure cannot, for man, be purely sensual, so, for man, mental pleasure cannot be purely spiritual. We may therefore, for our present purpose, abandon the dichotomy of matter and spirit and say all beauty is one beauty. And in the same way we may abandon the dichotomy of things and their purpose, for it is not possible for man, and it is not conceivable, to have one without the other. And so we may say that a good thing is a real thing and a real thing is a good thing. But as beauty is the conformity of the mind with things and their purpose, and that is to say the conformity of the true and the good, so we may say, [. . .] that the beautiful thing is the same as the real thing and the same as the good thing. But as the good thing is the real thing, and vice versa, so the beautiful thing is both. Therefore, as whatever is is true and whatever is is good, so whatever is is beautiful, and thus we may abandon not only the dichotomy of the true and the good but also the trichotomy of the true, the good and the beautiful.   NB215–7

8 The fact is, however, that we are artists because we believe in Beauty, and not that we believe in Beauty because we are artists.

What then is this Beauty in which we believe – what is its value [. . .]. Beauty is that order in things which we perceive to be in itself and at once both right and good. It is perceived by intuition, and the knowledge of it is developed by contemplation. Right – that is true to the nature of things and to its own nature. Good – that is well known, well done, according to the purpose of things and to its own purpose.

[. . .]

The knowledge of the nature of things must be enforced by the will to act accordingly. The true is the object of the intelligence, the good is the object of the will.

Suppose a workman has knowledge of his job and will to put that knowledge into practice (assuming that he has the necessary physical skill or tools – these things again having their own nature and goodness) the product of his labour is inevitably beautiful, and that beauty is immediately knowable and desirable.   AN102–3

9 Cave man with bone – the type of human artist.

That is the workman making a thing as well as he knows how and as well as he can.

Making a thing – i.e. not a picture of thing – not a representation.

[. . .]

Whatever view we take of the physical origins or development of men and animals, it is clear that there is a being called man – even if only a creature of the imagination. Even if I only imagine it – still I do imagine it – there is in my mind an image called man, and this creature (imaginary or otherwise) is one for whom beauty is the first need, not the last.

This is true of the most primitive conditions. In fact, the more primitive the conditions the truer it is – so true that there are in such circumstances no lectures about it and no [arts] societies. Man has not risen from depths of gluttony and avarice to the heights of beauty and disinterestedness in which we now find ourselves . . . rather it is that gluttony and avarice have overwhelmed him until he now finds himself in London or Liverpool. BLH70–1

10 Beauty consists in due proportion* and the word 'proportion' signifies the relations of part to whole and of whole to other wholes – as when one says of the human body that it is 'so many heads high' [. . .] – but beauty consists in DUE proportion and the word 'DUE' signifies a debt, so that to say that a certain thing has DUE proportion signifies that it has the proportion DUE to it – the proportion which it ought to have on account of its being what it is, and underlying the material (time and space) measure of things there is the spiritual (true and good) measure of justice.   AN148

11 Many [people] would no doubt answer that the difference between [what is art and what is not art] is that the former is beautiful and the latter is not; or perhaps that the cathedral is *meant* to be beautiful, was made beautiful *on purpose*, whereas the Forth Bridge is only beautiful, if it is beautiful, by accident; and therefore that the difference between *art* and *not art* is the difference between *beautiful* and *not beautiful*. Now this is really a very curious phenomenon because, as may be admitted, the word *art* does not in itself mean anything to do with beauty. We have suddenly and gratuitously introduced a notion of beauty.   WP8–9

12 Beauty has nothing to do with art! This sounds monstrous! Let us recollect ourselves. The object of art is right making (*recta ratio factibilium*). If things rightly made impress us as beautiful, well and good and so much the better. For the

*[St. Thomas, *Summa Theologica* 1, Q v art. 4 ad 1].

beautiful is 'that which pleases, being seen'. Beauty is simply the abstract name for that which pleases us – pleases by means of and through the senses. But beauty is not the object of making. Beauty is an accident of right making. Beauty is that which attracts us to the truth or what-not, just as beauty in cooking attracts us to good food and just as beauty in physical sensation attracts us to good action.   WP128

13 The criterion of art is beauty – not the moral character of the artist. I affirm, with the philosopher, that beauty is resplendent Being. I affirm that this property properly pertains to all the works of man, and that the fine arts are only distinguished from the useful arts as being those in which beauty is the object by definition, whereas in the useful arts the service rendered by the work seems to be the object.

I am content to let serviceableness remain the immediate criterion in the judgement of works of utility. I only demand that serviceableness shall be strictly criticized and utility taken in its widest sense.
[. . .]

I am content to let serviceableness remain the criterion in all works of utility because, apart from the fact that an industrialized civilisation can have no other, the feebleness of man's spirit, his proneness to self-aggrandizement, his sensuality, his silliness, always lead him astray. He cannot commonly be left to indulge his proper appetite for beauty unalloyed. Beauty comes to his work unasked when he works in a spirit of plain justice; when he considers simply the use of what he is making and the service of his fellows.

When it comes to things not merely physically useful, [. . .] though serviceableness may well still be the immediate criterion, it is not so easily applied.
[. . .]

– but what is the thing, whether of paint or stone or glass,
[. . .] What is the essence of this thing? What is its use to us?
What effect has the material of which it is made, and the
place for which it is made, upon its shape? [. . .] It is sufficient
[. . .] to state than when we judge, [. . .] whether by the
ultimate criterion of beauty or the immediate criterion
of serviceableness, our judgement is founded upon our
answers to these questions. If we deem that the workman
has understood these questions and answered them justly
in his work, then we deem his work good. Beauty is the
criterion, but we apply it, in such matters as architecture
and the painting or carving of images, without knowing it;
we are content to judge by the criterion of serviceableness,
knowing or being content with the assurance that, looking
after the good and true, beauty will take care of itself. For in
discovering what a thing is, we look after truth; in making
well the thing whose being is thus known, we look after
goodness; and beauty, which proceeds from goodness and
truth, is the resplendent though unsought reward.   AN294–6

14 Then when there has been clear understanding and affec-
    tion, combined with due knowledge and skill in the use
    of the materials and tools –
Then we shall call the work beautiful.
And we shall be tempted to say that beauty is a kind of
    radiance.
[. . .]
Indeed we may say that beauty is holiness – it is holiness
    visible.   SS68–9

VII

Of Imagination

1 The word image, curiously enough, for it is generally forgotten, means something imaginary, something seen in the
imagination. It does not mean simply something seen in a
mirror. The imagination is a faculty of the mind and the
mind is very far from being simply a mirror, [. . .] it
is a knowing and loving apparatus, and the faculty called
the imagination is not so much concerned to create veri-
similitude as to create visions of what is known and loved.
BLH96–7

2 The importance of the image is primarily the importance of
what it signifies, but in the making of the image, in its
material embodiment, there emerges another importance:
namely, the importance of the image as a material thing. It is
no longer merely an idea in the mind. It is a thing in this
world [. . .]. Did it exist as it should exist in the mind of man
who knows and loves and, now, does it exist as it should
exist in this place, in this stone? Was it as it ought to be in
the mind; is it as it ought to be in the stone? For as the mind
has its rights and wrongs so has the stone or the clay or the
bronze. What may be right in the mind may not be right in
flesh and blood, and what may be right in flesh and blood
may not be right in stone. And what may be wrong in one
may be right in another. So there is conflict, and give and
take, and a sort of marriage.

We hold, then, that things exist in flesh and blood and
these things are received into the mind*, and there they are
dwelt upon and transformed into creatures more suitable
to that mental habitation than things existing in ponderable

*['Nothing is in the mind but comes to it through the senses.' BLH101]

flesh can be. And because these creatures of the mind are
the fruit of love and there is 'great joy at their making – they
are not begotten betwixt sleep and wake' – because of this
love we turn again to the fleshly world, the world of stone
and wood and clay and metal, and recreate the mental
image, make it manifest, communicate it. This is the way the
common works of art are made – the way they have been
made for a million years – the way they are always made
where the mind is not tired and decayed.   BLH102–3

3 'Art imitates nature', as Aristotle said, but, as St. Thomas
Aquinas added, 'by working as she works', in *sua operatione*.
For the work of art is in its essence not a copy of something
seen with the bodily eye, not something seen as a photo-
graphic camera sees, not merely an imitation of the light
and shade and colour of visible things; it is in its essence a
translation into material of something seen inwardly, in the
imagination, a thing created first of all in the mind and then
reproduced in material. For though in a purely physical
sense of the word the imagination is nothing but a record-
ing and storing apparatus, there is another sense of the
word, the sense commonly implied when we speak as
human beings and not as scientists. In this other sense the
imagination is actually a creative power. No material thing is
known to us but by means of our five or more bodily
senses, but what comes out of our minds is not therefore
merely a material reflection or reproduction. For having
grasped a thing by means of our senses we then in a manner
digest it, turn it over and over, re-make it and re-form it.
However short this period of contemplation be, it cannot
fail of its effect. [. . .] But in the normal world we do not look
at things in order to measure them but to make them our
own, to possess them and in a manner to marry them and
thus make them fruitful. The resulting 'image' is in a real
sense a creation. For it is something which would not and

could not otherwise exist. It is not made out of nothing, but it is a new thing. It is the product of intelligence and will. It is the product of love. It is in this sense that we are made in God's image. For we are really creators. We do really make things which otherwise are non-existent. We create being where there was no being. For this indeed we were made – that we might collaborate with God in creating – that we might carry further his created world and carry it further in the direction of God Himself – that we might improve on nature by making things which are the product of love and not mere obedience. God Himself cannot make what we can make except in the sense that He made us in order that we should make things thus – that we should add to the material world things which are not only the product of His 'law' but also the product of our love and therefore of our love of Him – things which not only express His love of Himself but do so willingly and consciously, an echo of Himself and an echo self-returning.   DLvi–vii

4 So the created thing has four causes of existence, [see III.1] and there is first of all the creative imagination. To create: primarily, to 'imagine', as we say, what does not otherwise exist. For to take material and manipulate it to a certain end, to take wood and saw it in order to make a table, results in nothing unless the image of the table to be made exists first in the creative imagination. This image is the formal cause (as existing in the maker's imagination, the extrinsic formal cause; as existing in the thing once made, the intrinsic formal cause).   WP78

5 The [first Greek] sculptor's job [. . .] was not to make stone look like flesh and blood, but to make a stony version of a real person, a person he really believed in, and just because he was working in stone, and not in flesh and blood, he had to concentrate on the real nature of the God and not upon the merely transient accidents of the flesh.

He had to use his imagination more than his eyes. He had to imagine what the God really was, rather than copy his merely flesh and blood appearance. He had first of all to *believe* in the God, he had to believe in order to see. Instead of saying 'seeing is believing', he said: to believe is to see.   ISL131–2

6 [An image is] a projection of the imagination – it is the projection which is the art.

Most people can imagine things.

But art is Skill – Skill in making.

Art is the skill with which things are actually made. I don't mean technical dexterity as an end in itself. [. . .]

I mean technical dexterity in producing a material manifestation of the thing imagined.

The thing must first be imagined, and if it's a three-dimensional image, it must be imagined in this material or that.

Of course a man may say: I see the thing in my mind, but I don't see clearly what it's made of.

Well, that lack of clarity is a weakness, a weakness of the imagination.   MM107

7 Not to use the imagination is to be less than human. If the images it creates do not otherwise exist, then the agent or cause of their existence is responsible for their existence. And as the activity which produces them is an intellectual activity, to deprive people of it is to reduce them to a 'sub-human condition of intellectual irresponsibility'. That is the condition of men in our industrialism.   WP79

8 Production by machinery has produced the artist who is simply a designer. Every kind of work requires a designer because every kind of thing made is a thing made first of all in the imagination and someone must draw it out. [. . .]

But machinery runs according to the laws of mechanics

and not according to either morals or aesthetics. Therefore, the more purely mechanical become the functions of the workmen and the more purely mechanical his product, so much the more incumbent upon the designer is it to know and observe the laws of mechanics. The designer's imagination must conform to the machine. He must see machine-made things in his head.* ACC121

9 I want to keep the word 'art' down to the level of ordinary making & I want to exalt the workman to the high level of the imaginative maker. (I agree that in all ages many workmen have been largely unimaginative, but I think medieval conditions or say pre-industrial conditions made it possible for most men to develop at least a small degree of imagination whereas *our* conditions do the opposite and make 'imaginative making' more and more the sphere of special peculiar, 'abnormal' men.) I don't think in *our language* the word 'art' means only 'imaginative making'. There are too many words like 'artful' and 'artificial'. [. . .] I'd rather encourage a grave digger to think himself an 'artist'† than encourage a picture painter to think himself 'abnormal' – even abnormally imaginative – because I don't think it *is* abnormal to possess the rudiments of the power of

* ['Without the craftsmen there can be no design in that sense of the word which connotes aesthetic value. In this connection the engineer may be regarded as a craftsman, and the aesthetic value of his work is likely to be in proportion to its fitness for purpose. Unless the design arises out of the actual construction of the thing it is reduced to the level of extraneous ornamentation. Design, in fact, is inherent rather than applied and the "application of design" to mechanical processes suggests an attempt to get the best of both worlds by trying to secure the appearance of craftsmanship without its substance.' From a letter written by Edward Johnston to *The Times* circa. 1930 and quoted in Priscilla Johnston's *Edward Johnston*, (second edition 1976) p. 285. See also XI:13.]
† i.e. a responsible workman (and potentially an imaginative one). Would it not be possible to use the word *poet* more precisely to designate man as '*imaginative* maker'? Then I shd. say every man is potentially an artist & every artist potentially a poet.

'imaginative making' in spite of the tendency of industrialism to deprive the factory hand & the clerk of any opportunity of exercising that power.   LT293–4

10 Industrialism reduces the majority of workmen to a sub-
human condition of intellectual irresponsibility, and is
therefore an evil thing for the majority of men. It stunts
man's creative imagination. It allows men, the majority of
men, the use of creative imagination only when they are
not working, and therefore prevents the use of creative
imagination in the production of necessaries, and so all
necessaries are made by machinery and a quantitative
standard replaces a qualitative standard of life.   WL98–9

11 We may lay it down that the thing called an image is an
original product of the mind, of the mind informed by life
and work, by a life and work which involves intellectual as
well as moral responsibility. It is a product of knowledge,
not merely of information, and of love, not merely of
comfortable acquaintance. We make images out of what we
know, not merely of what we can copy by looking. We
make images out of what we love, not merely of what is
seductive or what has seduced us.

Such is the image in the mind, and it is the image in the
mind which is the object of the image maker [. . .] but the
presence of images in the mind is not only the result of
seeing but also, and more important, of thinking, willing
and loving.   BLH100–1

12 The imagination is the faculty by which what the eye sees
and what the mind thinks about it is re-created into what
the man loves.

That is why holiness is the ultimate test and ground of
good works.

For ultimately the holy is the only lovable – and ultimately only holy things are beautiful.   MM110

VIII

Of *Aesthetic Pleasure* and the End of the Fine Arts

1 If a thing has a certain form (and a material thing must have some form) the form must be the right form or the wrong, a good form or a bad, and when we say that a certain thing has right or good form we can only mean that it has the form proper to it if it really is what it purports to be. A profound sense of form means therefore a profound sense of what is right form, and that means a profound sense of what form a certain thing, being what it is, ought to have. But to know what form a thing ought to have involves the knowledge of what the thing that is to be made really *is*, and that involves knowledge of its significance and purpose, the place where it is to go and the material of which it is to be made. But knowledge of the significance and purpose of things is, for man, a rational and not merely animal being, conditioned by general as well as particular considerations, and it is precisely a profound sense of these general considerations, as well as of the particular considerations, which is necessary to the production of any good and right work.

If we deny that the forms of things owe anything of their quality of beauty, that is their power to please him who sees them [. . .] to the possession by their makers of some knowledge of what they were making and some good will in the execution; if we deny, that is to say, that good sense and good will have any part in the production of beautiful works; if we say that a thing can have good form and yet this good form, at least as regards its *goodness*, have nothing to do with what the thing is, then we are, in effect and in fact, denying that the thing we call beauty has anything to do with the mind, and therefore that beauty is simply a kind of visible or audible sugar, if we like things sweet, or a kind of visible or audible salt if we prefer them savoury. In such a view a beautiful man is not 'a man as he ought to be' (i.e. a man deprived of nothing that he ought to have – ugliness being simply privation), but is, as a thing of beauty, not a man at all, but simply a contraption of shapes and colours causing a charming physical excitement in the same way as does the light reflected in spilt petroleum.

This is no mean excitement, and I am not decrying it. Many physical sensations are highly delightful and only bad people regret it. But that this is *all* we mean or that this is what we *chiefly* mean by the word beauty is not to be believed. Let it be granted without any demur whatever, let it be granted with the utmost enthusiasm, that there is this physical kind of beautifulness. That is very good; but is that all?   BLH229–31

2 Aesthetic pleasure is grounded in the physical rather than the spiritual. Take, for example, music, which we make so much fuss about – concert halls, etc. Music, if it be separated from occasion (the wedding, the funeral, the feast, the march and the Mass) is, like modern abstract painting and sculpture, nothing but a titivation of the senses, and all that can be said of worshippers at the Queen's Hall is that they have possibly more refined tastes than those of children dancing to a barrel organ. But where-as the children, like new-born lambs, dance for exercise, the devotees of the concert are more like debauchees at a Roman feast – and if music entered the stomach instead of the ear, owners of concert halls would have to supply spumatoria. They have no *use* for music – they only want to enjoy it. Music as we know it today, in its latest develop-ments, is nothing but a refined sensationism, a refined debauchery, psychological auto-erotism à deux, à trois, en masse. The history of music during the last 400 hundred

years is the history of the progressive divorce of music from occasion, and the high talk musicians indulge in is no higher and no more precious than that which birth-controllers use to extol physical union. For music today, like married love under the inspiration of Mrs. Stopes,* is its own occasion. It sees no end outside itself. It is pleasure unalloyed. From Palestrina to Bartok and Stravinsky the history of music is a progress from meaning made attractive by music, through Handel and Gounod who straddled the fence, to music made attractive by meaning nothing at all. And what airs they give themselves and are given! And all this progress is entirely in line with the progress of industrialism – the divorce of work from beauty and of beauty from usefulness.

And now painters and sculptors are aiming at the same end. To mean nothing! Pure art, they call it. Pure beauty! And there are not wanting those who would make the art school a place for the encouragement of this aestheticism. Let no one accuse us of being indifferent to the appeal of high art. We have experienced its allurements. [. . .] The point is that all these fine feelings and fine sensations have got to go back into harness. In a machine civilisation these things are necessarily on the loose – divorced from necessary things they become hot-house flowers, man-eating orchids. Neither Sunday golf nor Sunday church can compensate for six days unhealthy work and six days 'business'. No amount of 'fine art' in leisure time can compensate for subhuman irresponsibility in working time. If necessary work is not made holy, recreation becomes idolatry.†
[. . .]

It is all thrilling, moving, exciting, titivating. If it is not so you feel defrauded – the thrill is what you pay for. The thrill

* [Marie Stopes, 1880–1958 amongst other things pioneer of a constructive birth control programme.]
† See XIV:13

is not a product of living, doing, acting, making, but of the isolation of the spectacle of those things and an intensification of enjoyment by means of that isolation. Just as the Stopesian lovers, freed from anxiety as to the consequences, are able more fully to *enjoy*, so the 'artist', freed by industrialism from the necessity of making anything useful, is able to concentrate upon aesthetic experience.
WP129–33

3 Nowadays, there is a lot of talk about feeling, about the emotions. What, then, are they, and what is their object? Is the capacity for feeling, the capacity for suffering emotion, a faculty of the mind and, if so, is it constituent to the pleasure we have in beautiful things? The roughness of language here again causes confusion; for the word 'emotion', like the word 'feeling', is commonly used in two senses and writers often fail to make clear which sense they are using. 'Feeling' means physical touching (as when we say, 'this apple feels rough'); it also means a kind of spiritual sensitiveness (as when we say, 'he has a feeling heart'). And 'emotion' has also the same twofold meaning. To produce an emotion may be either to produce a physical tremor of the nerves or an ebullition in the mind. It is obviously the mental senses which here concern us. The emotion produced by the sight of things may be merely physical or purely spiritual, or it may be both, and one may be mistaken for the other. The thrill produced by the hearing of music or the sight of nakedness, may be either physical or mental, or both, but in any case the thing called 'emotion' is a consequent, not an antecedent; what is antecedent is the mind – the intelligence and the will, the faculty for knowing truth, the faculty for desiring good, without which emotion cannot be suffered. We say the beautiful is that which, being seen, pleases; if we like to call this pleasure 'emotion', well and good, but we must make it clear that we do not refer simply

to that feeling of physical well-being which we call
'thrilling'.

Properly speaking, therefore, emotion is not a *faculty* of
the mind; it is a *state* of the mind; it is the state of a mind
whose faculties have been excited and, particularly, it is, as
the scholastics expressed it, the excitation of the appetitive
faculty, that is the will, the will which reaches out to the
good, which desires even the true because it sees it as good.
CL172–3

4 Art [. . .] no longer means *things* or the *making* of things; it
now means simply the exhibition of the worker's sensibility
and, chiefly, his appreciation of the *relations* of things. It is
now commonplace among the intellectuals to say that it
does not matter what things are, whether they are useful or
otherwise, appropriate or inappropriate: all that matters is
the relation between them. The visual relations between a
top hat and a mug of Guinness placed on a table are alone
of importance. Top hats do not exist, nor does Guinness's
stout. For the 'artist', the purveyor of fine feelings, the
presbyter of sensibility, the only thing that exists is the
effect of the appearance of those things upon his emotions,
that is to say upon his nerves; for he will not allow his
rationality to have any part in the business. The senses are a
kind of reason, said St. Thomas Aquinas, meaning that they
lead us to reality. But to the modern artist the senses do not
lead outwards to a real universe and a real God, but in-
wards to a more and more evanescent personality and
eventually to its real vanishing point.*   ACC124–5

5 The business of holding up a mirror to nature now means
holding a mirror up to the nature of the artist.   ACC108

* ['It is in making aesthetic pleasures, rather than pleasure in the intelligible
good, the end of art, that the modern "aesthetic" differs most profoundly
from the traditional doctrine; the current philosophy of art is essentially
sensational, i.e. *sentimental*. Coomaraswamy, op. cit, Vol. 1, p. 223].

6   The history of the private arts of the nineteenth century is a matter for special essays. How Baudelaire succeeded Wordsworth and converted the Wordsworthian study of man's reactions to sunsets into a study of man's reactions to his own state of nerves. How the business of the story-teller became less and less a recreation of things seen and things done and became more and more a reproduction of things felt by the writer – a revelation of psychology. For, as the work of the world became more mechanical, the lives of the people became stereotyped and, under police super-vision, sterilised. The only things remaining worth writing about were the interior mental adventures of the few re-maining unsterilized people, interlarded with descriptions of the few places remaining unmechanised. The factory has seldom been the subject of paintings and factory life seldom extolled.   ACC92–3

7   The modern artist is isolated; he is an eccentric. He has the same natural and normal incentive to creative activity; he has the same thirst for objective beauty, the same loves and hates; but he has not the same clientele. No longer is he naturally employed as part of the ordinary gang of builders or furniture makers. He is simply his own employer; there is no natural or proper place for anything he makes; the pedestal, the gilt frame, the concert hall, isolate him and his work from everything around it. It is not he who is abnormal; it is his age and circumstance.   AN285

8   The distinction between art and 'fine art' is, in every sense but one, a superstition – many superstitions are wide-spread, so the mere popularity of the distinction need not concern us. [. . .]

   The idea that the distinction between art and fine art is that art is skill applied to the making of useful things and fine art is skill applied to the making of things of beauty, is clearly unreasonable – because there is no reason why useful things should not be beautiful, and there is no reason to suppose that beautiful things have no use. Are tables and chairs and houses and pottery necessarily ugly? Are portraits and statues and church paintings and wall decorations necessarily useless?

And the idea that the beauty of useful things is accidental whereas, in the fine arts, it is the usefulness that is accidental, is equally unreasonable, for you cannot have beauty by itself, any more than you can have art or culture by themselves.

[. . .]

But there is one sense in which the distinction between art and fine art is a possible one, and that is when we distinguish between the necessary arts, the arts necessary to the business of living, and the arts of *recreation*, the arts whose purpose is mental and physical recuperation – so that we return again to the arts of living, revived and refreshed.

[. . .]

But even though the distinction between the arts of living and those of recreation is a valid one; and apart from the fact that such a distinction only makes the fine arts more useful than ever (for what is more useful and good than something which enables us to return to work refreshed?), even so, it is obvious that the distinction is one of category: a scientific division rather than one of nature.   SS93–5

9 In order to disarm the criticism that a world in which all men's aesthetic sensibilities were kept in harness to necessary work – in which the idea of art as being essentially useless, [. . .] in which the idea of 'art for art's sake' was expunged from the state and in which, therefore, all the concert halls were demolished as well as all the art galleries, in which music no less than painting and sculpture returned again to their allegiance, one might even say their proper

bondage, to necessary work [. . .] I say in order to disarm the criticism that such a world would be one devoid of the highest and noblest expression of man's spirit there is this to be said: it does not appear to be a fact that greater heights of human expression have actually been reached in the modern world, or in the very similar periods of decadent Greece and Rome, than in those periods, whether in medieval Europe or in India or China or Mexico or Central Africa, during which aesthetic experience was subordinated to and harnessed to necessary works. The sculptures of Chartres, the paintings of Ajanta, the idols of Tehuantepec or Gamboon and the subtle melodies of the ecclesiastical Chant reach heights of expression at least as great as is shown in the works of any individual master or 'old master' we can name.   WP133–4

10   'In the beginning was a thought, not a thing', and therefore it is that intelligibility is the final cause of all things. 'Pleasure perfects the operation', but is not the object of working. Final happiness consists in the joy of knowing and not in the satisfaction of sense however refined. Nevertheless, we must not under-value or eschew pleasure as though it were evil. On the contrary, exactly as in our physical life, in eating and drinking and all other bodily activities, when there is no pleasure in the work we know there is something wrong with it, and when there is nothing pleasing in the result we know it has been badly done, so it is with things made – pleasure perfects the operation. And there is even pleasure in pain when the pain is the necessary accompaniment or companion of good work. Thus there is satisfaction in the pain of ordinary physical labour and, in the heights of holiness, there is pleasure in the agony of maternity and of martyrdom. 'A man should have joy in his labour,' says the Preacher, 'and this is his portion'; nevertheless, art remains a rhetorical and not an aesthetic activity.   LE10–1

11 Consider that industrialism [. . .] – as we know it. The diabolical direction in which it is going – on which it actually prides itself – is the supersession of human labour in the necessaries of life by the machine. If they win, human labour will be only for hobbies – (fancy work, fret-work, 'pure art' they call it – art released from utility. 'Industrialism has released the artist from the necessity of making anything useful', and it has released the workman from the necessity of making anything at all – the machines will do the making – man will only mind the machines). The necessaries of human life – the things men need and therefore love, the things upon which, during the countless centuries of human history, men and women have expended all their care and skill and pride – the arts of agriculture and the farm, the arts of the kitchen, clothes, furniture, pottery and metal, the whole business of building – from cottages to cathedrals – all these things will be made or done by machines, and we shall be released for 'higher things'. So they say. But for the majority of men and women – for us – there are *no higher things.* If, as it says in St. James' epistle, 'true religion and undefiled is to visit the fatherless and the widows . . .' then we may also say, this is true art – *to make well what needs making* – for love of God and for the service of our fellow men and women. And again, to keep ourselves 'unspotted from the world' – that is, the world of flattery and vanity and personal display, and exhibitions, and museums, and art galleries and art critics, and all art nonsense.   WP139–40

12 To hell with culture, culture as a thing added like a sauce to otherwise unpalatable stale fish! The only culture worth having is that which is the natural and inevitable product of an honourable life of honourable work.   SS173

IX

Of Slavery and Freedom

1 That state is a state of Slavery in which a man does what he likes to do in his spare time and in his working time that which is required of him. This state can only exist when what a man likes to do is to please himself.

That state is a state of Freedom in which a man does what he likes to do in his working time and in his spare time that which is required of him. This state can only exist when what a man likes to do is to please God.

A man is a slave when between him and God who is the *final* cause is interposed another man as an *efficient* cause.

A man is free who is subject only to those causes which are called final. In as much as man is a material body he is subject to efficient cause – as a stone is moved by a kick, i.e. the kick is an efficient cause. In as much as man is a living spirit he is subject to a final cause – as when a man and woman are married at a church and not at a registrar's office, i.e. the Church is a final cause.

We are not slaves because we are subject to final causes, but only when we submit to another person as an efficient cause.

The test of a man's freedom is his responsibility as a workman. Freedom is not incompatible with discipline, it is only incompatible with irresponsibility. He who is free is responsible for his work. He who is not responsible for his work is not free.

Efficient management and 'scientific' organisation (e.g. the factory or servile system) are certainly conducive to the comfort of the worker (slave) and to his steady employment and security. There is not necessarily anything materially uncomfortable in a state of slavery and there is not necessarily anything materially comfortable in a state of freedom.

That man is by nature free (i.e. by the will of God) is a religious affirmation (i.e. not to be proved – whether by reference to history, which, indeed, might easily be made out to show exactly the contrary, or by any other means). There is nothing to be said against slavery except that it is not the will of God. There is nothing to be said for freedom except that it is the will of God.

The service of God is perfect freedom.   AN1–2

2 That a man may show the love of God in his work he must be free. A factory hand may show the love of God in his life or in his thought – he cannot show it in his work. The work-man has as much right to make and to act upon an aesthetic judgement in his work as he has to act upon a moral judge-ment in his life, or as he has to make an intellectual judge-ment in his thought. He has also the right to choose the authority to which he will submit in any of the three spheres, but no man has the right to compel his sub-mission. Only God has such a right, and God has given man free will!   AN4–5*

* ['The lowest order of Homeric society was the serf. Homer introduces us to one of them, the swineherd Eumaeus. His condition is not without honour: he is "famed" and his epithet is "divine". He is treated with respect by his lord, the king; he has the courage to retort to a nobleman and does so with impunity . . . We who have seen the caste system at work know that a serf receives honour, because he is a kind of priest and sometimes represents gods. We know that the record of that system is not one of unmitigated oppression, but on the contrary it can be far less oppressive than our industrial system. Its machinery works far more smoothly because it is amply supplied with the oil of etiquette. The lowest owe service which in theory they cannot refuse, but no one can compel them to render it with a will; they can only be heartened to it by giving them whatever honour is their due, . . . Their privileges have to be respected, and at the same time prevented from extending unduly. Heredity, so far from placing them at the mercy of their master, puts him in their hands; for you can dismiss a hireling but not a hereditary servant,

3 It is well nigh impossible to determine what human acts are
   not, in fact, determined.

   The crux of the question of free will is the responsibility
   of men for the choice which follows deliberation. But it
   remains undiscoverable whether the choice really follows
   on the deliberation or was actually made before it and, if
   made beforehand, determined by habits, instincts and in-
   heritances allowing no interference. In spite of this puzzle
   we know ourselves to be responsible and would rather be
   responsible than not.   NB40

4 I am only saying that all must make a decision. And our
   decision involves *belief*. You must *believe* in responsibility or
   deny it. You may allow an unlimited – unlimited because
   undefined and undefinable – amount to the sphere of
   determined actions, while at the same time claiming that
   freedom and responsibility exist all the same. Or you may
   deny freedom and responsibility altogether. Whichever
   you do, you must believe; you cannot prove.   NB41

5 What is wrong with men who disbelieve is not that they
   cannot but that they will not believe. The defect is in their
   wills.   NB28

6 I do not so much *think* I have free will as *believe* it, and I act
   according to that belief whatever my limited powers of
   thinking may prove one way or the other. The word 'belief'
   is therefore a very much stronger word than 'think'. When
   we use the word 'think' we imply a possibility of error. But
   when we use the word 'believe' in its proper manner we
   admit no such possibility. To think is to use our powers of

---

so if you want to reap peace and good service you must sow tact and
good manners. Hereditary service is quite inconsistent with the ruthless
industrialism of our times, and that is no doubt why it is painted in such
black colours.' A. M. Hocart, *Caste*, (London, 1950) pp. 139–140.]

reasoning upon facts as known to us by observation or experiment or by hearsay, that is to say, information received. Thinking is obviously therefore liable to many kinds of error. [. . .] To say 'I believe' is, however foolishly or foolhardily, to rise to the affirmation of certainty.   NB14

7 Man is a complete person. He has free will. [. . .] And because the will is free it may be perfect.

It is possible to be perfectly willing (that is why they say that 'the service of God is perfect freedom').

We cannot be forced to will what we do not will or to desire what we do not desire.

But it is not possible to be perfectly knowing. I might be perfectly willing to write this essay. I cannot say I know perfectly what I ought to say.

Hence emerges the [. . .] principle:

that will is perfectible, but not knowledge.   MM119

8 But when we consider the question: Why do we do what we know to be wrong? It is not other people's wrong-doing that is in question but our own; and although the findings of science, of psychology and all the rest, apply to us as much as to other people, we know, we affirm, I know and I affirm that at the very core of our being, of my being, there is the fact of responsibility. We may not be able to say why such and such an appetite is so particularly strong, or such and such another so particularly weak, but we do know that we are creatures meriting praise or blame.

The question then: How did sin come into the world? is answered by saying: It came in with free will. If free will is a fact, then it explains the possibility of sin.   NB218

9 It is significant that the rising of what we call modern science synchronized with the throwing off of spiritual authority. We have deliberately thrown off the 'easy yoke' and 'light burden' and have placed ourselves under the

hard taskmaster of immutable and impersonal 'laws of nature', and this has been done in the name of freedom. [. . .] The highest virtue we can attempt to claim is a stoical courage in the face of a meaningless concatenation of fortuitous circumstances. Such is the freedom of the sons of science.

[. . .]

Our fault has been that we sought freedom – we found an iron law of causality. We sought free-thought – we found psychological determinism. We sought free love – we found that we had lost Love itself. Dear silly sheep, we have lost the Shepherd and found only the wolves.

The only freedom we did not seek we have deliberately thrown away. We did not seek for freedom of the will. [. . .]

We have thrown away free will. We do not like to be held responsible. We like to be treated as animals, automatons. When the psychologist says, 'it is heredity, it is early environment, it is a complex', we applaud. When Augustine says 'it is sin', we deride. The word 'sin' has become almost meaningless; it has become a sentimental word like 'art'. [. . .]

As the idea of responsibility pervaded all men's works and all their deeds, so does our idea of irresponsibility. We have erected, as is natural, a system of industry exactly corresponding to our philosophy and depending upon it. *Actus sequitur esse*. We do not believe men are responsible; we have made them irresponsible. [. . .]

And in the world in which the man of money is king the workman is nothing but a tool. It is common knowledge: the workman is only a tooth on a wheel. What he makes with his hands is not his responsibility and its only concern to his master is its saleability. And as these irresponsible tools are the great majority of the population, they provide the biggest market for the sale of the things they produce. Therefore saleability is that quality in things which makes them attractive to irresponsible tools. By the introduction of machinery the quantity of things made is increased a hundredfold and the responsibility of the workman reduced to nothing. His power to discriminate between good and bad is completely lost and in the end it has necessarily come about that the only things which it is possible to sell are those which no intelligent person finds it possible to buy. [. . .]

There is no remedy but that which man alone has power to apply. And every individual must first apply it to himself. He must reclaim the one freedom he has thrown away; and he must throw away all the other freedoms he has falsely claimed. He must reaffirm the freedom of his will and his consequent responsibility for all his deeds and works. He must reaffirm the reality of sin and himself a sinner. Then shall we be free – 'with the freedom with which he has made us free'.   ISL11–7

10 The service of God is perfect freedom – perfect freedom is to be perfectly bound. God himself is perfectly free – he is perfectly bound to himself – he can be and love nothing but himself. And we are free when we are his, of him and bound to him.   ISL10

X

Of Work and Responsibility

1 The type of the free workman is the artist, and the artist
is, by definition, one who is concerned with the Absolute
Beauty. The Absolute Beauty is God. The artist is concerned
with God. As the priest brings God to the marriage, the
artist brings God to the work. All free workmen are artists.
All workmen who are not artists are slaves.   AN5

2 'Love God and do what you will.'* [. . .]
    Many people are afraid of the words 'do what you will'.
They think they sound like licence. But in fact they are
thoroughly well safeguarded by the other two: 'Love God'.
The loving of God cannot be done by those who refuse to
recognise the voice of conscience. The voice of conscience
must be silenced by those who use tyranny and injustice.
Modern conditions of employment prevent men, even
those who love God, from doing what they will. This is
tyranny. It is a crime of injustice. Modern conditions are
unjust.
    It is said that the essential perfection of a watch is that it
keeps time. That is true of watches made in factories,† for
watches made in factories are, in effect, not made by men at
all, inasmuch as no man can be held responsible for making
them. Man is made by God and lives in that relationship.
Things made by man must necessarily have that relationship also. Man is responsible to God for what he makes, and
the essential perfection of a man-made watch is the love
of God to which it bears witness. No man can be held

* St. Augustine.
† Factory: a place where things are made, in which the individual workman is not responsible for the design or workmanship of the thing
made, being only responsible for doing what he is told. [. . .]

responsible to God for a factory watch because no man can be held responsible for making it!   AN10-1

3 But the point here is this: that by setting up a system of production in which no workman has any responsibility for the form or quality, the intellectual quality, of what he takes part in making, we have set up a system essentially evil, the product of which cannot by any stretch of imagination be called christian. It is evil because it is contrary to the nature of man. Its product is unchristian because Christianity did not come to destroy but to fulfil the law of nature – because the law of nature is the law of God.   AN270-1

4 Does the development of machinery and of machine facture tend to develop our souls and supply us with objects more and more truly conformed to our nature as creatures who know and will and love [. . .]?   CMA57

5 It is abundantly clear, after a century and a half of industrialism (and it is coming to be admitted on all hands), that only when they are shorn of all the human business which characterized the products of the pre-industrial world, and only when thus shorn, can machine-made things be tolerable.

   To be good, machine-made things must be inhuman in kind – yet it is for the use and environment of human beings that they are made!

   Were we only making pig-troughs for pigs, and did not so much as see them ourselves, then there might be less reason for criticism – at least the things made would be good and suitable, even though the human beings who made them were deprived of any occasion to praise God in their works and were deprived of any but an indirect means of serving their fellow-men, but it is not so.

   It is not solely for the service of animals that the industrialists offer their system, and yet their system is unsuitable for any other service.   CMA59

6 The real distinction between tools and machines is discovered in the sphere of control and responsibility. Who is responsible for the thing made or the deed done? – and deeds done, when viewed in themselves and not simply as means to ends, are also to be regarded as things made. Who is responsible for the thing made?   NB88

7 A society which preserves among its people a strong sense of responsibility (for responsibility is the concomitant of free-will) and at the same time a clear notion of good (and a knowledge of good is bound up with a knowledge of truth; for you cannot will what is good without knowing what is good) – a society which preserves among its people a high level of responsibility and a clear notion of goods to be willed, will be a society in which the arts will develop strongly and it will be a society in which all ordinary workmen, as well as the more intellectually gifted ones will be, in a true sense of the word, artists – that is 'responsible workmen'. The people, in fact, will be 'artistic' – history, both written and that which we preserve in museums, proves this conclusively.   BLH141–2

8 Everything made by free workmen has the quality of original form, that is to say, it has a form for which the maker is responsible.   AN254

9 The thing, then, that I have called 'original form' is essentially a matter of order, ['as God reduced chaos to order, so men in past times have given the quality of order to the things they made'] it is the 'splendor formae' of St. Thomas, it is the shining out of Being, it is the thing called beauty. And to achieve it men must will it, and to will it they must be free. The free man is responsible for what he does, but for the work of a slave another is responsible. That is the whole difference between the modern workman and his counterpart of past times. The modern workman is not

responsible for doing anything but what he is told. The modern industrial system needs tools, not artists, and a century of industrialism has destroyed in the workman the very memory of artistry. With this destruction it has come about that beauty has ceased to be the common quality of things made, for under the factory system, with its concomitant machine production, no man can be held responsible; and therefore to conscience, which is essential to the production of things of beauty, no appeal is made. The only thing which is considered is the satisfaction of the consumer, the buyer. AN256

10 Greatly as we have dishonoured and corrupted and destroyed the arts and crafts of men, reducing the workman to a 'subhuman condition of intellectual irresponsibility', the root of the matter is in the dishonouring of physical work, and until we have eradicated the prevailing notion that some kinds of work are, of their nature, subhuman drudgery, all discussion of human labour is futile. LE26

XI
Tools or Machines?

1 First of all we must make it clear that we understand the distinction between *tools* and *machines*.   SS102

2 The real distinction between tools and machines [. . .] is that tools are instruments by means of which we *do* things, but that machines are instruments for *making* things.   NB88

3 As the machine demands in the operative a virtue of the will (conscientiousness and good will) or a sharp eye in the overseer, before the mechanical product can secure the technical perfection which is not only proper to the machine but its chief reason for existence, so the response of the craftsman's tool to the control of his hands demands in him a corresponding virtue. But this virtue is one of the mind, judgement. Those are in error, accordingly, who suppose that when the craftsman strives after technical excellence he is emulating the machine standard. And those are even more grievously mistaken who suppose that if the craftsman neglect his responsibility to exercise good judgement and skill in the actual performance of his work, the consequent lack of uniformity [. . .] will give to his work the vitality or liveliness which is characteristic of hand work.   TY98–9

4 Here, perhaps, is the key to the problem. It is something to do with human responsibility: anything is a tool which you use to help you to do anything. Anything is a machine in so far as you help it rather than it you.

   Thus, for the carpenter and the sculptor, a chisel is a tool.
   But, at the other extreme, an automatic box-making apparatus is only a tool in a fanciful and deceptive sense,

for it does not help anyone to make boxes; it actually does the making itself, and the industrialist and his men help it to do so. The men help it by minding it and oiling it; the employer helps by keeping the men fed and warmed. The men, in fact, are simply sentient parts of the machine. They have no responsibility whatever for the form or quality of what the machine turns out. Nor has the industrialist any responsibility except in so far as he has it in his power to scrap the machine and get another if it does not make the kind of boxes which he wants.

[. . .]

Tools then are helps to men, but men help machines, and that is the difference.

Of course, the matter is complicated by the fact that there are innumerable sorts of apparatus, and that the line between tools and machines is difficult to draw.

[. . .]

Nevertheless, the distinction is clear in principle.

If you are responsible for the form and quality of the thing made, then whatever apparatus you use is a tool rather than a machine. And as that responsibility diminishes so the apparatus becomes more and more a machine until the point is reached when, as with the latest automatic machinery, the machinist has no responsibility whatever and becomes simply a machine himself, a robot, an instrument paid for by his employer as part of the cost of production.   SS102–6

5 You can if you like, call tools machines or machines tools, but you cannot say there is no difference between doing things the way you intend and doing them the way the designer of the machine or tool intends. If I take a piece of iron and with my fingers and various tools (or machines if you prefer the word) shape that iron into the shape of a box, *because that's the kind of man I am* – that is one thing.

If I take a similar piece of iron and put it into one end of a machine (or tool if you prefer the word!) and it comes out at the other end a box, *because that's the kind of tool or machine it is* – that is quite another thing.

[. . .]

The test is always the relation between the work done and the man doing it. If the shape and quality of the things produced are matters for which the workman is responsible, that is one thing; if he is not responsible it is another.   ACC115–6

6 [The] tool gives the maximum of control with the minimum of distraction. It is most important that the workman should not have to watch his instrument, that his whole attention should be given to the work. A sculptor does not see his hammer and chisel when he is carving, but only the stone in front of him. Similarly the hand press printer can give his whole attention to inking and printing, and hardly sees his press. [. . .] It is not a question whether machine work be better or worse than hand work – both have their proper goodness – it is simply a matter of difference.
TY96–7

7 Whatever we may think of machinery in itself and as an agent for the production of things desired, we must re-member its two-fold origin – the growth of capitalism and the dispossession of the peasantry. Machinery as has frequently been said, was not invented to make things better or even to help the workman. It was not introduced either by the workman or the designer of things to be made. Its origins were neither humanitarian nor artistic, but purely commercial.

[. . .]

The purpose of machinery was to save the labour which would have been required to make the vast quantities of things for which they envisaged markets and which, in the absence of machinery, would have been altogether too costly to produce. That supply of labour was available. It had been made available by the landlordism which succeeded feudalism. What the avarice of merchants did not supply was supplied by the avarice of the new landed gentry.   ACC80

8 It was perhaps inevitable that the history of machinery should be what it has been. It is difficult if not impossible to imagine any other chain of circumstances than those which actually occurred which could lead up to such an accumulation of capital as was necessary to make the invention and construction of machinery possible.*   ACC79

9 It is perfectly possible to make good things by machinery. It is perfectly possible to make works of art in a proper sense of the word. But to bring this about it is necessary that the machines shall be owned and controlled by the designers of the things to be made. That is the thing which the historical introduction and ownership of machinery has not allowed. Machinery was not introduced by the workman in order that a different kind of thing, a machine made thing, might be made. It was introduced by men of business solely that money might be made and for no other reason whatever.   ACC78

10 Machinery [. . .] does not, in fact, exist to make things at all [. . . but] to make the thing called profits.   MM57

* 'The Protestant Reformation, for example, is far more a political than a religious event, and cannot be understood apart from the struggle of the rising bourgeoisie against the confinements of Feudalism. The Catholic Church in the Sixteenth Century was not only incomparably the greatest of Landowners, but was the ideological backbone of the feudal system, nationally and internationally. In England especially, the plunder of the Church played a big part in that primitive accumulation of capital without which the modern industrial world could never have come into existence.' *New English Weekly*, Jan 4, 1934, p. 285.

11 It is with reference to the things made that the question of
machinery is chiefly of importance here. And it is precisely
the things made which have been machinery's main failure.
They have been failures for the simple reason that no man
of business can afford to be disinterested.* Men of business
are necessarily at the mercy of the undisciplined fancies of
those who buy things and the undisciplined desire for
money of those who advance the capital. Between the
capitalist and the consumer the man of business is between
the devil and the deepest part of the Atlantic Ocean. The
growth and multiplication of joint-stock companies has
developed in the investor a frame of mind morally in-
distinguishable from that of the usurer pure and simple.
The spread of machine industry on commercial lines, and
competition between rival manufacturers has brought it
about that the buyer's fancy is the only test commercially
applicable. And the buyer being, in the majority of cases,
himself either a factory hand or a clerk in the business
has no standards by which to judge the good quality of
anything.   ACC81–2

12 It might be urged, why all this to-do? Why not let the whole
thing 'rip' as heretofore? [. . .] Why bother to do by reason
what the process of time and man's natural tendency to the
true and the good will do in any case? [. . .]
    It is not true of human works that they are, like the dam
of the beaver, the product of the blind instinct of animals.
Man's works are primarily the product of his ideas and of

---

* ['Disinterested', we would remind the reader, not 'uninterested'. Thus the
workman is impartially free to consider only the good of the work to
be done if he is to succeed as artist/maker. Moreover, 'it is the business
of the artist to *know how things ought to be made* and to be able accordingly,
as it is the business of the patron to know *what things ought to be made*, and
of the consumer to know what things *have been well and truly made* and
to be able to use them after their kind'. Coomaraswamy, op. cit, Vol. 1,
p. 80.]

his imagination. Influences which have borne upon his mind have always changed the kind and quality of his works. It is indeed impossible to say at any point: here is the product of reason untouched by instinct; for man is an instinctive animal as well as a rational soul, and in any particular work reason and instinct impinge upon one another and the work is a product of both; moreover, man's consciousness is underlaid by his subconscious and acts which are not consciously reasoned are not necessarily simply instinctive. But to say that there is no need to appeal to reason, that things will right themselves without any such appeal, is precisely the doctrine which in four centuries of Protestantism has brought us to the present mess.

ACC113–4

13 Just as an ordinary sensible man may sometimes do silly things, so an admirable machine may be the instrument for making imbecilities.

And just as man may do unnatural things, things contrary to his nature, properly understood (for strange as it may seem to some philosophers, we hold, with Aristotle and others, that everything has its proper 'nature'), so a machine may be used, or even designed to make something contrary to the nature of machinery.

The simplest example of this kind of imbecility is the use of machinery to do what we call 'ornament' and the designing of machines to make 'ornaments'.

For, however little we recognise the fact, ornaments are 'in their nature' a kind of ikons. They are objects of worship; they represent what we consider, in however small a degree, lovely and lovable and holy. CMA50

14 If the use of ornaments is personal, so also is the making of them.

For the use of ornaments is a mental or spiritual one, and

the mental or spiritual is not patient either of dialectical exposition or of exact measurement.

It is therefore impossible to state precisely what shape or size is correct; it is only possible to give general rules.

Each separate image or ornament is only, and cannot be more than, an approximation to the truth, and thus all good art must be of its nature experimental.

I cannot say precisely how you can or should use an image of the God of Love.

You cannot say precisely how I can or should make one. You can and should give me directions; but you cannot say my prayers for me.   CMA54–5

15 [Nevertheless] men may have pleasure in well-made factory products [. . .]. For though a good machine-made article does not exhibit all possible goodness – it does not, for example, exhibit the goodness of charity, of tenderness, of sweetness; in short, it does not exhibit the goodness of humanity – nevertheless it exhibits all the goodness that is possible to it, it being what it is – a sub-human production – the product of men who, willingly or unwillingly, have submitted to the discipline of the factory. [. . .] But sub-human things are not in themselves bad things. They may serve their purpose. And the man who sees them may see their functional suitability and be pleased by the sight.

And such functional suitability is, in its degree, holy. For it is logical and to that extent, it is good.

It fully satisfies the ratiocinative side of man's nature. For man is reasonable as well as wilful and, confronted by useful things, even if they are merely useful, he does not suffer the misery he suffers when confronted by the absurd, the illogical, the unreasonable.   WL118–9

16 The whole of our trouble is the secularization of our life, so that we have descended to an animal condition of continual struggle for material goods. By sin – sin, that is to say,

self-will and self-worship – by sin man does not descend from the superhuman to the merely human, but from the superhuman to the sub-human. Strange fact! Man cannot live on the human plane; he must be either above or below it. The marvellous feats of our mechanized 'scientific' industrial world are not human feats. They are no more than the feats of highly intelligent animals and the more we perfect our mechanization so much the more nearly do we approach the impersonal life of bees or ants.   AU282

XII

Of Man, Manufacture and Industrial Nemesis

1 There is something wrong in our society – [. . .] something
   radically wrong. How can such corruption fail to affect our
   art and industry? How can a discussion of art and industry
   fail to concern itself with the radical evils of our time? It is
   not window-dressing we are concerned with, but the very
   basis of human industry and production.   LE88

2 God has made the world and he has made man such that
   labour, that is to say, work, is necessary for life, and God
   cannot have made necessary that which in itself is bad.
   Moreover, as Solomon, inspired by the Holy Spirit, said: '. . .
   nothing is better than for a man to rejoice in his work, and
   this is his portion.'*

   Now it follows from these things that nothing which truly
   subserves our life can be bad, and therefore there can be no
   form of necessary work which is in itself degrading. In these
   latter days we have to be more than usually clear in our
   minds about this. The idea is prevalent that physical labour
   is a bad thing, a thing to be avoided, a thing from which we
   may rightly seek release. We cannot discuss the question of
   work, the question of the factory system, of the machine,
   of the arts, until we have right notions as to the nature of
   physical labour itself.   LE21–2

3 Our object is to rebut the common belief, which industrialism must necessarily encourage, that, [. . .] *'manual
   work is, of itself, subhuman drudgery'*. This is not only untrue but
   subversive of the whole christian doctrine of man. Un-
   fortunately, in the circumstances of our industrial world,

* [Ecclesiastes, 5.18–19.]

nothing could seem more obvious common sense. When we consider the working life of the millions of factory-hands, of shop assistants and clerks, of transport workers, and of the agricultural labourers on our degraded farms, it is obvious that much of the work is, indeed, sub-human drudgery and it cannot but seem a good thing that, by the use of machinery, at least the physical pain has been eliminated.

[. . .]

It should be obvious that it is not the physical labour which is bad, but the proletarianism by which men and women have become simply 'hands', simply instruments for the making of money by those who own the means of production, distribution, and exchange.

[. . .]

We must return again and again to the simple doctrine: physical labour, manual work, is *not* in itself bad. It is the necessary basis of all human production and, in the most strict sense of the words, physical labour directed to the production of things needed for human life is both honourable and holy. And we must remember that there are no exceptions.   LE24–5

4 Drudgery is not inherent in the nature of the work, 'of itself', but in the sub-human conditions consequent upon commercialism, industrialism, and the abnormal growth of cities.   LE27

5 Judged by a quantitative standard and, as regards many of its products, from a qualitative one also, this industrialism receives universal approbation. [. . .] There is at present no wide-spread discontent with the system itself, inhuman and anti-human though it may be. Not only are the quantitative advantages obvious to all, not only are certain desirable things produced by machinery which otherwise are un-obtainable [. . .] but the system is now so 'dug in' that it

would require a quite impossible revolution to bring about a return to pre-industrial manufacture. [. . .] industrialism is with us, no one wants its abolition; why, then, is there so much discontent and misery?   SS160–1

6 The fundamental trouble with industrialism is that it provides unlimited goods for consumption but provides, of its own nature, no education for consumers. In the very process of industrial production the education of the consumer is destroyed. For industrial workers form the mass of consumers, [. . .] and industrial methods of production reduce the worker, as the theologian puts it, to a subhuman condition of intellectual irresponsibility. [. . .]

   The best education is production*. The best education industrialism of its own nature can achieve is an education in unquestioning obedience to processes over which the workers have no control.   MM20–1

7 The control of industry by people to whom the main object of industry is the profits accruing to them as private persons poisons, corrupts and degrades both the product and the producers. And the chief victims of this evil thing are the workers, for not only is everything the product of labour, but labourers are the majority of the users.   SS191–2

8 Our industrial commercial empire has achieved a thing never before achieved in the whole history of the world. It has achieved a division of the human race never before attempted – a division not of rich from poor, not of free from unfree, not of good from bad, clever from stupid but, unique marvel! a division of artist from workman. ACCvii–viii

9 If we say that the object of man's existence is man's salvation and that the object of Christianity is to promote man's

* [See footnote to XI:11.]

salvation and that the Church exists to promote Christianity we may go on to say that the only question of any importance in any sphere of activity is whether or no this or that thing is or is not consistent with Christianity.

[. . .]

It is necessary, perhaps, to be clear about the word 'consistent' and not confuse it with the word 'compatible'. For many things are compatible with Christianity which are inconsistent with it. Thus slavery is not incompatible with Christianity but is undoubtedly inconsistent. A man may be a slave or even a slave-master and yet be a Christian, just as a man may be murdered or a murderer and yet be a Christian. A man may even be a good Christian and yet be a slave-owner or a murderer if by some strange chance it has not been brought home to him that slave owning and murder are inconsistent with Christianity; and a man may be a very good Christian and yet be a slave, for though, in the slave, rebellion may be a virtue, for some slaves rebellion is too difficult.

If, then, it be said that such a thing as a factory or the Factory System is inconsistent with Christianity, it must be clearly understood that that is not saying that a man who works in a factory cannot be a Christian; nor is it saying that a factory owner or one owning shares in a factory or one buying or using things made in a factory cannot be a Christian, for in all these cases the relationship of the soul with God may be good and right and beautiful and the factory is simply a material circumstance the evil of which is not recognised. [. . .]

The factory system is unchristian primarily because it deprives workmen of responsibility for their work. A factory 'hand' is not responsible for the work he does.

[. . .]

The modern factory system is as servile and even more unchristian than the pagan system of slavery. The pagan

slave-owner merely owned the slave's body. In the absence
of a factory system of workshop organisation the slave's
mind was, in practice, his own and the work done by slaves
was often of a kind for which each slave was in a high
degree actually and personally responsible. The modern
factory system is a refinement on the ancient slave system,
for in the factory system the workman's mind is owned by
the master, while his body is legally free. Thus the Christian
tradition of opposition to physical slavery has been dodged
and the master has been able to reap all the benefits of
slavery without any apparent violation of freedom. But
the violation is coming to be recognized on all hands and
especially by the workman himself. The so-called 'labour
unrest' is not, as the masters would have us suppose,
entirely due to the unbridled greed of the workmen and
their appetite for high wages. It is really due to the workman's instinctive, if inarticulate, desire for freedom and
responsibility and if it chiefly takes the form of a demand
for high wages and shorter hours, this is only a case of
'the biter bit', for higher profits and longer holidays is
the chief ambition of the masters. The worship of money
is a worship which the workman has learned from his
superiors.
[. . .]

It is a Christian principle that every individual soul is
responsible and not irresponsible. It is Christian teaching
that the first human activity is the love of God and the
glorifying of Him. It is not sufficient that God be glorified by
faith; it is equally necessary that He be glorified by works.*
The modern system of factory production deprives men of
the power to glorify God in their works and of the responsibility for so doing. Therefore the Factory System is evil and
damned.   ISL19–24

*['Even so faith, if it hath not works, is dead, being alone'. James 2:17.]

10 The value of the creative faculty derives from the fact
   that that faculty is the primary mark of man. To deprive
   man of its exercise is to reduce him to subhumanity. [. . .]
   The value of the creative faculty is that its use enables
   man to save his soul – for without that faculty he has no
   soul to save. You cannot save the soul of an automaton;
   for an automaton has no saveable soul. [. . .] When the
   catholic priest says, 'a man can be a very good catholic in
   a factory' he is of course speaking the exact truth . . . But
   it remains true that a man is as out of place in a factory as
   in a lightless dungeon, and that as continuous darkness
   atrophies the eye so continual intellectual irresponsibility
   atrophies the creative faculty and makes men less than men.
   WP84–5

11 Our industrial system [. . .] simply separates, divorces, the
   material and the spiritual. That is what is meant by 'original
   sin'. Original sin is the loss of original integrity, so that what
   God willed to be united man tries to put asunder. Original
   sin is the disintegration of human personality. [. . .] The
   attempt to divorce art from work and use from beauty is not
   new. It has been made from the beginning and resisted
   from the beginning. You may not believe in the resurrec-
   tion of the body, you may not believe in original sin, but
   both doctrines are the necessary corollaries of the fact that
   man is matter and spirit, inseparably both. The separation
   of matter and spirit, matter and mind (for mind, including
   all the faculties of the soul, the memory, the understanding
   and the will, is another name for spirit), is man's death, and
   industrialism leads so clearly towards that separation that
   we may say death is the actual aim of industrialism, its
   diabolical direction. Thus have human values been attacked
   since the beginning, and thus did the nineteenth century
   with its commercial rule and its industrialism make its
   characteristic and almost decisive assault upon them. The

values of humanity are those which have their sanctions in human nature.   NB264–5

12 And if the time come when machines have been so perfected as to need no human guidance or supervision, or at most only a few hours by a few men per day, even so Industrialism would still mean that necessary things, houses, furniture, clothes and food, things which during all the centuries of man's history have been his chief means for pleasing himself, his only means of collaborating with God in creating, would be deprived of that beauty which is the special mark of human work, the beauty of tenderness and sensibility in the actual handling of material things. ACC95–6

13 Industry means labour as such, the simple exercise of strength. It requires persistence, but not necessarily love, or initiative or imagination or creativeness – and therefore nothing specifically human or personal.   SS3

14 'The dignity of labour' is a phrase having no meaning in an industrial society. Or, if any meaning still attaches to it, it is but the dregs of the meaning it had in what you might call Old Testament times. The labour of a shepherd in the lambing season, the labour of the ploughman, of the mason, of the maker of sacred images – all such labours are venerable, and venerable because of a dependence upon the personal will and reason of the labourer. So also is the labour of the housewife. Such labours are responsible for the form and quality of what their deeds effect. Such labourers are persons. And as persons they serve their fellow men.   LE83

15 If all necessary things are to be made by machinery and with as little human labour as possible (for this is admittedly a necessary corollary), then we shall be deprived of any necessity to serve our fellow-men.

Such bodily labour as will be required must inevitably be State planned.

Such morals and culture as our governors deem desirable must inevitably be State-given and State-controlled.

And instead of the whole of life being based upon the necessity of personal service – the service of men by one another – and pleasure the proper accompaniment of work well done, and done as befits our humanity and a heavenly destiny (as is the accompaniment of eating and drinking and procreation and all other natural exercises), there will be no need of personal service, and pleasure will not be the accompaniment of work, but the very end for which we shall live.   CMA66–7

16 These things being understood, there is no suggestion in anything I am saying that I think it possible to put back the clock or that we can become Ancient Britons . . . It is, in fact, no more possible to go back than it would be to go forward in the direction of an even greater and more complete mechanization of industry. My position is merely that of one who happens to see what that direction is and what is its end . . .

No, there is no putting back of clocks. The clock of our civilisation will run on.

[. . .]

The decay and eventual disappearance of industrialism is inevitable. The motive which sustains it is not man's vocation to holiness, and holiness is necessarily the ultimate value in human affairs.   LE84–5

17 Industrialism is of its nature a business of large scale machine production. Of its nature it is a business of public service. Of its nature it is not private ownership. Of its nature it means the regimenting of the majority of workers both technically and as citizens. Is it not obvious then that the claim to private profits from public services is

preposterous and can only be made by fools or knaves? Is it not obvious that the capitalist, profit-seeking control of industry cannot much longer continue? Not only are men corrupted but the production also is degraded. Competition for markets, the obsession with salesmanship, the gambling and scrambling on the stock market, the necessity every small man of business as well as every large one is under of thinking of everything in terms of buying and selling – these things corrupt the nation. As St. Thomas Aquinas says:

> 'If the citizens give themselves to trading, a way is open to many vices. Since the desire of trading tends especially to gain; therefore, through the use of trading avarice is enkindled in the hearts of the citizens; the result being that in the city all things will have their price; mutual trust will be at an end, doors will be opened to fraud, the common good will be despised, private good will be sought, zeal for virtue will wither . . .'*

SS184–5

18 Considering the history of the last three hundred or five hundred years, ask yourselves whether the control of politics by people whose one aim in working is the making of money, can be good for politics.

Ask yourselves whether the division of human beings into two classes, the responsible and the irresponsible, the people who control and the people who are controlled, a minority who do what they choose and a majority who have no power of choice, can be a good thing.

Ask yourselves whether it can be a good thing to divorce the useful from the lovable, the necessary from the delightful, the artist from the workman.

Ask yourselves whether it can really be in accordance with the nature of man and his end that what he does to earn a living should be regarded as something to be got over as quickly as possible in order that he may have more leisure.   WP76

* De Regimine Principum, ch. 3 trans. V. McNabb, O.P.

XIII
Property, Ownership and Holy Poverty

1 The ill from which we are suffering is the decay of
personality. The remedy is the revival of personal property.
Under industrialism the majority of the people are deprived of personal control of their work, and such control
is impossible without ownership. What you do not own
you cannot control. What you do not control you are not
responsible for. If you are not responsible you cannot be
either praised or blamed. Christian doctrine lays it down as
a first principle that man has free will and is, therefore, a
responsible person – master of his acts and the intended
consequences of his acts. This doctrine is flouted and
denied in our society. In all but name England is a servile
state.

The irresponsibility of the workman is the first and
simplest way in which to see our evil condition. It is the first
because the exercise of work is the formal reason of individual appropriation.* It is the simplest because the exercise
of work is within the experience of all but a small class of

* ['The work of art has been pondered before being made, has been
kneaded and prepared, formed, brooded over, and matured in a mind
before emerging into matter. And there it will always retain the colour
and savour of the spirit. Its *formal* element, what constitutes it of its kind
and makes it what it is, is its being controlled and directed by the
mind. . . . Artistic work therefore is specifically human work as opposed
to the work of the beast or the machine; and for this reason human
production is in its normal state an *artisan's* production, and therefore
necessitates a strict individual appropriation. For the artist as such can
share nothing in common; in the line of moral aspirations there must
be a communal use of goods, whereas in the line of production the
same goods must be objects of particular ownership. Between the two
horns of this antinomy St. Thomas places the social problem . . .' Maritain,
op. cit, pp. 7 and 150.]

persons. But though it is the first reason, the exercise of
work is not the only reason of personal and private ownership. The second, and depending on the first, is the security
and dignity of the family.   LE34

2 At the root of all our arguments for the institution of
   property is the fact that man is a person, and he requires,
   therefore, not merely food, clothing, and shelter as such,
   but that particular food, clothing and shelter which is conformed to his unique personality. And parallel, as it were,
   with that fact is the fact that the material world into which
   he is born is such that only by his personal deliberate manipulation can material be made conformable to his needs.
      There is only one necessary thing which is obtainable
   without deliberate labour, the air we breathe; all other
   necessities are in one degree or another the product of
   labour. If men were not persons, possessing proprietary
   rights over themselves, mastery over themselves and over
   their acts, it would be possible to feed, clothe, and house
   them in herds and regiments and hives, and the claim to
   personal and private ownership of the means of production
   would have no rational ground. [. . .]
      Now, physical and mental labour upon the earth and
   upon raw materials is the primary necessity for the
   preservation of human life. We may now go farther and we
   may say that as the object of human life is man's sanctifi-
   cation, labour being the means of life is the appointed
   means to holiness and thus to beatitude. It should be clear,
   therefore, that of all kinds of ownership, that of the means
   of production is the most important, and so important is it
   that, as Pope Leo XIII says, it is a natural right, natural, that is
   to say, in accord with the will of God; it is God's will for
   man. We have, therefore, two things to bear in mind: the
   necessity of labour, and the consequent natural right to
   property. The one follows from the other; for it is man, a

person, who must labour and 'the very essence of this activity is to imprint on matter the mark of rational being.' (Maritain)   LE29–31

3 Man is matter and spirit and the mind of man is both intellectual and moral. The right to property follows from man's material necessities and his intellectual nature. The right to property is not primarily a moral right, a right due to man on account of his free will but is, so to say, an intellectual right, a right due on account of his intelligence. The right of ownership does not derive from man's need to *use* things but from his need to *make* things.

As a moral being, purely as such, man has no right of private ownership. On the contrary, as [. . .] St. Thomas Aquinas says:

'With regard to external things, a man ought to possess them not as his own but as common, and always be ready to put them at the disposal of others who are in need' (*Sum. Theol.* 11–11, 62, 2).

It is to man as workman, as an intelligent being who must manipulate things in order to make them serviceable, that private ownership is both necessary and a natural right. Only when there is full control of the means of production can there be proper and suitable manipulation. Unless I own the fields I cannot exercise my skill and intelligence upon the land. (It is for this reason that ownership is better than tenancy and that, in the case of a tenant, the terms of tenancy must be as nearly as possible equivalent to ownership). Unless I own the stone and my tools I cannot properly exercise my skill and intelligence as a stone carver. [. . .] It is this necessity of manipulation which gives the right of private property in the means of production.   LT358–9

4 When I say that the farmer, the craftsman, should own his own land, workshop, etc., I do not refer to that quasi absolute ownership which goes today by the name of

'freehold'. Ownership means control, personal control, but, definitely, control for good not evil, not for private aggrandisement but in the interests of society and the common good – in the interests of the individual also, but of the individual as a member of society; [. . .] Absolute ownership, implying a right to destroy or misuse or leave unused what is necessary to the good of others, is an evil myth. Therefore the ownership I mean is a tenancy, hereditary if desired, granted by responsible authority, enjoying the support and defence of public opinion and law, but implying specified duties and obligations as much as rights and carrying with it no opportunity for the exploitation of other people.   LT394

5 It is because of the necessity of manipulation, without which no natural product is of service to man, that there is the necessity of private ownership. And it is because the service of men implies good service and not bad that an artistic problem merges into and becomes a problem of morals. It is immoral to deprive men of what they need. Men need goods, but in order that goods be made well there must be individual appropriation of the means of production. It is thus that the denial of private property becomes a breach of morals. But the immorality is not due to any direct injustice or lack of charity, but indirectly, because while in the order of *doing*, of prudence, of service to one another, the use of things should be in common, in the order of *making*, and for the sake of the things made, ownership must be private. Where there is no private ownership in the means of production there is injustice, and therefore a breach of the moral law, because the quality of things made or of services rendered is reduced and men are deprived of what is due to them.   WP108–9

6 No such problem existed in pre-industrial times. [. . .] By a 'pre-industrial age' [. . .] I mean that primitive state which

has existed everywhere where workmen owned the means of production and which exists still in every place where men still do so. Such a state existed in England in the seventeenth century – more or less – never quite perfect, but still sufficiently perfect to strike a note – so that you could say: here is a country in which the means of production, at least the tools and materials, are owned by workmen – that is the kind of country it is. And in such times intellectual discipline was imposed, as well as moral discipline, by the ordinary work. For a man was responsible not merely for doing what he was told, but also for the shape and quality of the thing he made. And he was disciplined also by the fact that he dealt personally with the buyers and users of the things he made. It was inevitable that his work should be both intellectual and moral education.   WL47–8

7 For it is only as persons that we serve one another, and when personal control is divorced from ownership, it is only with great difficulty that men retain responsibility for the form and quality of what is done or produced.   CMA34

8 Ownership is necessary to human happiness, to human dignity and virtue, and ownership means control. A share in the profits is not ownership. Money in the savings bank is not control of the means of production. The only desirable and at the same time the only possible reform of our world is distribution of ownership.   SS168

9 Ownership of profits is the worst feature of our present world. To make everyone capitalists, to implant in the minds of every worker the capitalist, profit-seeking motive would be to extend the disease to all. Is that what is wanted? SS192

10 'As many as possible of the people should become

owners'* – as many as *possible*. Who are the possible owners, using the word possible to imply not merely the physically possible but also the spiritually possible? For many things are physically possible against which the mind revolts, and that against which the mind revolts is, in the long run, impossible, even physically. [. . .] The only possible owners of the means of production under an industrial system are the workers collectively. [. . .]

Neither can it be argued that the means of production could be owned by consumers as such and in their collectivity. Consumers have not the means of judgement between good and evil. They can only judge whether things are good for *them*. They can only make relative judgements. But the maker, the worker knows what is good in itself.†
SS194–5

11 But ultimately the most important fruit of individual appropriation, of private property, is the exercise of charity. We are responsible persons, responsible for what we do and for what we make. To what end is this doing and making? [. . .] 'that he may have something to give to him that suffers need,' says the apostle. [. . .]

'Something to give' – that is the primary thought and the last word. In the word 'give' we have the key to the whole problem. Whether it be the workman who must give himself for the good of the work to be done, or the parents who must provide for their children, or all of us who must live in love and charity with our neighbours, in every case economic freedom is necessary to support and make materially effective the precepts of the Gospel. Only upon this basis can a christian society be built – a christian society, that is to say, a society of free men united in and by the love of Christ – free men, that is to say, men who enjoy the

* [Leo XIII, Rer Nov. Par. 35.]
† [See XI:11 and its footnote.]

ownership of land and workshops, who own not merely
themselves but the means of production. For you cannot
give what is another's. You cannot give yourself if you are
a slave. [. . .] 'Faith without works is dead,' but our works
cannot be good works unless they are our own.   LE35–6

12 Another and ultimately more important reason for individual appropriation of the means of production – so
important as completely to obliterate any other – is the fact
that only when men own the means of making is it possible
for work to be what it is meant to be, the praise of God, a
song of praise, a sacrifice of praise. Praise is its real and only
enduring reason of being,* and to that end, much more
than to the end of human service, individual appropriation
of the means of production is necessary.   WP112

13 I must put before you a principle which is of primary and
permanent importance [. . .].
  That principle is the principle of POVERTY.
  But first of all I must make it clear that I am not speaking
of destitution, want [. . . not] the evil poverty endured by
men and women who are denied their just human needs.
  I am talking about poverty as a *good* – just as chastity is a
good and obedience is a good. I am talking of that poverty
which as the theologians say, is 'the rational attitude in a
material world, that virtue which regulates our attitude to
material things'.† I am talking of *holy* poverty, which is
that same virtue strengthened and inspired by love. That
poverty which is a necessary good, the poverty of the spirit
which is the crown and seal of the Kingdom of Heaven, that
spiritual poverty which, like all spiritual things, bears its fruit
in human life and works, and must bear fruit or perish.
  But it is only in love that this poverty can be embraced –
like that chastity – like that obedience.

* [See also VII:3.]
† [I have been unable to trace the source of this quotation.]

[. . .]

   . . . the teaching of poverty. *To go without, to give up, to lose rather than gain, to have little rather than much* – that is its positive teaching.   LE86–7 and 91

XIV
A Vision of Normal Society

1 The activity of man is directed to an end. That end is contemplation – theologians call it 'the beatific vision'. Man's
final end is God. All his activity in his earthly life is directed
towards that end. The attainment of that end is the goal of
all his doings. Art and prudence, religion and politics are
only to be explained thus. There is no rhyme or reason
otherwise in human life. Whatever is done, whatever is
made, must be criticized as being in harmony with that end
or as discordant with it. To set up a perfectly organized state
is only reasonable if such a state is conducive to man's final
beatitude. Human pleasure, the pleasure we have in good
things, in using good things, knowing good things, seeing
good things (and the word seeing includes all the other
senses – but seeing is the best sense to name because it is
the most obviously connected with man's rational nature) I
say, the pleasure we have in good things is only explainable
and only endurable if and when and because it is a foretaste
of beatitude – it is a mark and a sign and promise of our
divine destiny – our heavenly home. [. . .] all man's earthly
activities are directed towards his final bliss.   WL73–4

2 At the break-up of the medieval system two great disrup-
tions were acting and inter-acting – the Reformation and
the Renaissance. At the beginning of the fifteenth century
the class of persons now called artists did not exist, nor was
there such a thing as an architect's profession. There were
simply various grades of workmen, skilled and less skilled,
well known and honoured, or unknown and unhonoured.
But the present distinction of classes among workmen was
entirely undeveloped.

The modern distinction between the working classes, the middle classes and the upper classes was not to be found. There was a thing very different – different in its origins and in its effects. There was distinction of functions. There was no such thing as the gentleman as such or so called. The King was honoured as king, the Bishop as bishop, the Farmer as farmer, the Knight as military leader, the Mason as worker in stone, the Merchant as collector and distributor of goods, the Money-Lender as Jew, but no one honoured simply as gentleman or dishonoured as merely workman. It is unnecessary here to develop a treatise upon the social institutions and ideals of the middle-age. What is necessary is to show the effect of the loss of the Catholic mediaeval idea of functional distinction, as opposed to class distinction, upon the practice of the arts. And yet it must not be supposed that the idea of that time is something peculiarly either Catholic or mediaeval. It would be truer to say that it is simply humanly normal; that it was fostered by the Church rather than invented by her; that its almost complete victory was lost on account of sin and pestilence rather than by the uprising of other and equally good and normal things.   AN226–7

3 It is an abnormal condition of things wherein we differentiate between ordinary workmen and artists. The normal differentiation is simply between one kind of artist and another. Thus in a normal human society a mason and a sculptor of images are simply different kinds of artist. The violent distinction of artist and not-artist could hardly exist among workmen in such civilisations as those of Rajput India or mediaeval Europe. Even in England the normal condition lingered up to the end of the eighteenth century, and in out-of-the-way places untouched by mass production and the factory it is still to be found. And, as among ordinary workmen, the makers of ordinary utilities, the

distinction between artist and non-artist does not normally exist, so in a normal state the distinction between art and 'fine' art is only made with difficulty, and is more of a philosophical distinction than a practical one. Sculpture and the making of furniture are both jobs in which due regard should be paid to the way the thing, image or table, ought to be made. And who will say that, whereas an image ought to be beautiful, a table need not be so? The conscious effort after beauty is categorically the thing which distinguishes the fine arts from others; but why deny such a conscious effort to one kind of workman and not to another? As practical people and people who suffer from the over-developed self-consciousness and introspection of modern 'artists', we may well complain that there is altogether too much talk about beauty. We may say: 'Look after goodness and truth, and beauty will take care of itself,' and, applying the Gospel, we may say: 'He that loseth his life shall save it,' as much in art work as in the work of salvation.   AN281–2

4 The abnormality of our time, that which makes it contrary to nature, is its deliberate and stated determination to make the working life of men & the product of their working hours mechanically perfect, and to relegate all the humanities, all that is of its nature humane, to their spare-time, to the time when they are not at work.   TY8

5 We artists represent the normal man, the maker of things. For us this age is less dazzling. And the modern world, though it give us titles and estates, though it pamper us and spoil us and flatter us, can only refuse us the one thing we hold desirable. It can give us an honoured place – it cannot, even if it would, give us an honourable job.   AN191

6 Scientists have got to come off their high horses. The fact remains: art is a normal human activity as scientifically

controlled industry is not; for making things by human means for human use is the normal occupation of human beings, while the quantitative mass production methods which are the natural consequence of the scientific method are in their nature abnormal and sub-human. Art as a virtue of the practical intelligence is the wellmaking of what is needed – whether it be drain-pipes or paintings and sculptures and musical symphonies of the highest religious import – and science is that which enables us to deal faithfully with technique. As art is the handmaid of religion, science is the handmaid of art.   LE15

7 This excessive subdivision [of mechanised production] is inevitable where profit-making is the motive. It is, however, the artist and the workman who are to be blamed, not the man of business. The man of business does his job very well. Certainly he has his no right to be ruler, as he is at present, but it is our fault for allowing him to rule. And as good men must precede good law, and not vice versa, so the individual must revolt against the evil system and not wait until the many are prepared to revolt with him.   AN98

8 My contention is that [. . .] we've got to make the best of modern conditions – no crying over spilt milk – and that the best will be made when all agree together to start with sheer reasonableness, continue with honesty, and let the end be what it may.   LT209

9 I am only concerned to discover man, to disclose him. It seems obvious to me that if we could answer such a question as: 'What is man that thou art mindful of him?' and if our answer were generally accepted as the right one, and not only accepted but welcomed, we should not find the difficulty we find today in our multitudinous disagreement. Agree about meaning and the rest follows. A political form will be conceived to correspond with the accepted

end. Let man rediscover his norm and he will recreate
normal politics and a normal society. It is the abnormal
that must be planned beforehand – the bureaucracy,
corporative or communist; the tyranny, military or capitalist.
NB352

10 Though a unanimous society is primarily defined as one in
which there is unity of mind among its people, and therefore unity of religious observance, mental unity is not its
only characteristic. Religious unanimity pervades such a
society in all departments of its life, and determines and
colours not only social custom and behaviour, law and
commerce, but also the whole business of agriculture,
clothes, building and furniture, and from the meanest art of
the crossing sweeper to the most final achievements of
poets and architects, painters, sculptors and musicians,
there is an indwelling conformity of mind pervading, informing and forming all things. Of nothing can it be said
that it 'doesn't belong'. In such a society it is no more
possible to discover a boot or a spade that is 'out of keeping' with other things than to find a religious or political
opinion at variance with the communal mind. And in such
a society this binding and informing power is a spiritual
one.   NB341–2

11 We deceive ourselves when we discover or think we
discover a satisfying beauty in the works of even those
societies which, moved by unanimity, are also moved by a
unanimity of what seems to us the highest type, the most
humane, the least barbarous. We may discover, and we do
often discover, a beauty beyond our comprehension and
beyond our emulation. We see the sculptures of Chartres or
the paintings of Ajanta, Apollo of Tenea or the church of the
Holy Wisdom at Constantinople, and, remembering that
these works are as much the works of the whole civilisation
in which they sprang as of the actual workmen who made

them, we are momentarily tempted to say: there, there was heaven on earth; there, there man arrived at fruition, at happiness, at fulfilment; O, that we were there . . . But this is deception. Even such beauty is not our beauty, and we know that we would not return to any past century in the expectation of perfect happiness, nor find in any country delight unalloyed. Those works are not really what we desire; they are but reminders of it. They reflect or show forth the desirable reality, but they are not it. It is that reality which we must find, and, having found, portray. And that portrayal, though in the making of it we love it as a thing to be loved for its own sake (and thus even the maker of walking sticks or toothpicks, if he is to make them well, must make them as being images of the God and sharing the God's worship), is to be known simply as furniture, useful furniture, the fitting furniture of a civilisation directed heavenwards. Thus and thus only we shall escape the snare of desiring religion for the sake of art, for we shall no longer desire art. The artist will be simply the honest workman.
NB346–7

12 Throughout human history culture has been the product of the work men did for their livings.   BLH203

13 The Leisure State is founded upon a false angelism, a false notion of the fitness of men to enjoy themselves without the direct responsibility of each one to earn his living and that of his wife and children by his own work [. . .] It is the notion that matter is essentially evil and therefore work is essentially degrading. [. . .] that is the basis of our Leisure State – the release of man from his entanglement with matter. The highbrow exponents see it in highbrow terms – higher things, high art, beauty, contemplation . . . Ordinary people are not thus constituted. For them it means simply a release from drudgery and insecurity, from slum-life and overcrowding, from underfed and unhealthy children. It

means more travel in motor-cars, at greater speeds, more racing, more football matches; in fact, more of everything but of that dreary business which industrialism has made of work – of which no one could be expected to wish anything but to see the last of it.

[This false notion] has no foundation in a generous spirituality. It is not the product of an overwhelming love of God, as though one should say with St. Paul: 'I long to be dissolved and to be with Christ.' Far otherwise! Here is no desire for the pure bliss of some beatific vision; here is nothing but a desire for release from drudgery and privation. [. . .] no idea more noble or even more human than to have *a good time*. For, don't you see, in the Leisure State people won't really *love* the 'good things' they will enjoy in such plenty. They won't love them in the sense that they will see them and use them as *holy* things, things in which and by which God is manifest. In reality they will despise everything. Things will be made only for passing enjoyment, to be scrapped when no longer enjoyable. [. . .] It is all a great illusion; the release from work does not and will not mean the love of a good life and of good things; it does not mean the City of God; it means, at the best, an impossible angelism and, at worst, an impossible aestheticism, the worship of the pleasure of sensation.
LE70–2

14 From one point of view the townsman is right. It is a lot of nonsense all this cackle about the beauty of the country. And the cackle would never have been heard if the towns had not become such monsters of indecency and indignity. The right and proper and natural development of human life unsullied by an insubordinate commercialism no more leads to ugly towns than to an ugly country side. On the contrary, the town properly thought of is the very crown and summit of man's creativeness and should be the

vehicle for the highest manifestation of his sensibility, his love of order and seemliness of dignity and loveliness. Man collaborates with God in creating – that, physically speaking is what he is for. The natural world, following, without the slightest deviation, the line of least resistance, blooms in a million million marvels of natural beauty. The beauty of flowers and trees and beasts and insects, the beauty of bones and muscles and crystals and clouds, is product of this unswerving but unconscious obedience. Man alone among created things can resist: man alone can willingly obey. Man alone can give thanks: man alone can respond and take a conscious and willing part in the universal creativity. Thus, properly thought of, man's works, alone of all material things, can have the spiritual qualities of tenderness and love, of humour and gaiety: and they alone can, on the other hand, have the qualities of wickedness and pride and silliness.   AU231–2

15 Let us but understand this: Man knows himself as a being and not only as a doing and a becoming. Even the professing materialist knows it, though he will not admit it. And, so knowing himself, man demands inclusion in the author of his being, Being itself, God. And, as in the body, the members are subject to the head as directing, so in human society the members need a head to which they may be subject and a body of which they are the members. Men are the members of this body and they are beings. The head also must be a being [. . .] Therefore, as the head is the lord of the body, so Being itself, God, is the lord of all beings. And as man is incarnate, so it is fitting that Being itself should put on incarnation. And the Word was made flesh.   NB353–4

Epilogue

The end is the beginning and that, in the end, is what we shall discover to be the first thing which it is necessary to believe. What possible and desirable ends can fructify our imaginations and inspire a formality? I say God is man's final cause, and why should I let the reader off more lightly. He can do his own 'letting off', and the best way to make the burden light is to discover what the word God connotes and, in the process, to weed out all that it does not. I do not intend to let the reader off more lightly because all seemingly lesser burdens turn out to be more burdensome.

NB336

A NOTE ON THE LINDISFARNE PRESS

The Lindisfarne Press publishes books in many fields, including history, literature, philosophy, science, sacred science, religion and art. It also publishes the *Lindisfarne Letter*, the journal of the Lindisfarne Association, recent issues of which include such themes as: *Celtic Christianity*, *Homage to Pythagoras*, *The New Biology* and *The Evolution of Consciousness*. The Lindisfarne Press also provides an extensive mail order catalogue service in order to make available not only its own books and tapes but also hard-to-find publications and 'tools for cultural renewal' in many different areas. For further information, please write: The Lindisfarne Press, R.D. 2, West Stockbridge, Massachusetts 01266, U.S.A.